Horst Bredekamp

SIGMUND FREUD'S FIGURAL PSYCHOANALYSIS

Horst Bredekamp

SIGMUND FREUD'S FIGURAL PSYCHOANALYSIS

Michelangelo's *Moses* and the collection of idols

Translated from the German by Elizabeth Clegg

DE GRUYTER

Published with the support of the Cluster of Excellence „Matters of Activity. Image Space Material" funded by the Deutsche Forschungsgemeinschaft (DFG, German Research Foundation) under Germany's Excellence Strategy – EXC 2025 – 390648296.

Title of the original German edition:
Horst Bredekamp: Sigmund Freuds figürliche Psychoanalyse

ISBN 978-3-68924-244-2
e-ISBN (PDF) 978-3-68924-044-8

Library of Congress Control Number: 2025945217

Bibliographic information published by the Deutsche Nationalbibliothek
The Deutsche Nationalbibliothek lists this publication in the Deutsche Nationalbibliografie; detailed bibliographic data are available on the internet at http://dnb.dnb.de.

Cover illustrations: Left – Max Pollak, *Portrait of Sigmund Freud*, 1914. Etching. London, Freud Museum. © Freud Museum London. Right – Michelangelo, *Moses*: torso, arms, hands, beard, Tablets of the Law. 1513–15. Marble. Rome, San Pietro in Vincoli. Credits: Jörg Bittner Unna, CC BY 3.0, https://creativecommons.org/licenses/by/3.0, via Wikimedia Commons.
Typesetting: P. Florath, Stralsund
Printing and binding: FINIDR, s.r.o.; Česká republika

www.degruyterbrill.com
Questions about General Product Safety Regulation:
productsafety@degruyterbrill.com

A NOTE ON THE ENGLISH TEXT

The content of this English publication adheres to that of the German volume published in Basel in 2023, with the chief exception of one longer passage (comparing Sigmund Freud and Arthur Schnitzler as collectors), added towards the end of Chapter II, and four shorter passages (each elaborating on the pre-existing text), added to Chapter III. Minor factual and typographical errors have been corrected in the course of making the German-to-English translation. The purpose of other slight textual adaptations is to ensure that the author's intended meaning is clear to the reader. The Bibliography, now extended by a further thirty entries, has been re-worked so as to cite every publication in its original form. Sigmund Freud is himself the focus of a four-part segment within the overall listing. The Index replaces a register of featured individuals.

EC. London, June 2025

TABLE OF CONTENTS

ACKNOWLEDGEMENTS

German edition, 2023

Many people played a part in the conception and preparation of this book. Martin Beck, Marie Egger, Anina Gröger, Raphael Hoffman, Nike Meiners, Emily Oberkönig, Kolja Thurner and Kay Usenbinz have provided sterling assistance with its organisation, including the procurement of both literature and images, and a critical reading of the text. Nike Meiners prepared the register of featured individuals; and Marie Egger devised the annotated plans of Freud's consulting room and study at 19 Berggasse. Christoph Baron has brought his incomparable editorial eye to a reading of the entire text. None of these contributions would have been possible without the support of Humboldt University's Exzellenzcluster Matters of Activity.

Tatjana Bartsch supplied me with source material relating to Ludwig Pollak; and Andreas Bayer, Kerstin Germer, Jörg-Dieter Kogel, Ulf Jensen and Barbara Wittmann provided valuable advice on a great many points. I was fortunate in being able to discuss with Peter Schäfer the consequences of my reflections for the history of religion. Sybille Moser-Ernst and Werner Ernst have evinced a touching loyalty in their readiness to debate with me, both in person and in correspondence, numerous aspects of my thesis and my arguments. Without their critique and their advice this book could not have come about. Finally, Christfried Tögel has generously helped to rid the text of errors – those of my own making and those to be found in the literature – and has, in addition, provided a wealth of information, some of it drawn from as yet unpublished research of his own. At the very last moment I was able to profit from Felix Jäger's kindness in agreeing to examine my text.

The invitation I received from Gottfried Boehm to speak in Augst, near Basel, and the resulting introduction to Schwabe Verlag, gave rise to the impulse for this publication. I am most grateful for the care that this publisher – and here, above all, Arlette Neumann and Jelena Petrovic – has taken in the production of this book.

I extend my heartfelt thanks to all those I have named. The experience of scholarly collaboration at its best equates to more than the sum total of many cases of gratefully received assistance; it attests, rather, to an instance of shared empathy – in itself a rare phenomenon – oriented towards a single objective.

English edition, 2025

I am both pleased and thrilled that my study of Sigmund Freud's "figural" psychoanalysis should now – after its translation into Italian and into French – appear in an English edition. Not only was this a language well known to Freud, as witness the range of his reading and his correspondence. It was also that in which he "made his home" from June 1938 and his forced emigration from an annexed Austria. Freud's cherished collection of "idols" (itself central to my concerns) was soon re-installed at his new, London address, which is now that of the Freud Museum. I am deeply grateful to Petra Florath for the energy, the intelligence and the visual flair she has brought to devising the overall layout of this volume. The English version of my book owes much to Elizabeth Clegg: to her talents as translator and editor, and to the wisdom she brought to appraising the original, German text. For all of this I extend my most appreciative thanks.

HB. Berlin, June 2025

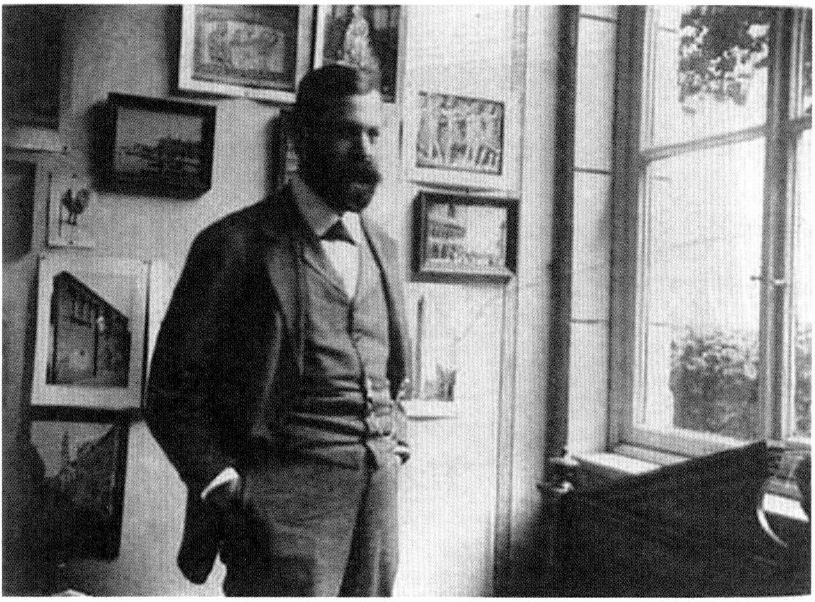

1| Alexander Freud, "At the historic corner window", 17th June 1897. Photograph. London, Freud Museum

INTRODUCTION: FREUD'S "GREAT VEILING"

The photographic portrait of 1897

Alexander Freud was a passionate photographer. One of his shots shows his famous elder brother, Sigmund, posed "by the historic corner window", in daylight entering from the right (Fig. 1).[1]

This photograph was taken in Alexander's room in the house of their mother, Amalia, at 14 Grüne Thorgasse in Vienna.[2] Erect, yet with hands concealed in his trouser pockets, the subject is posed so as to avoid any hint of formality. Behind Sigmund is a wall on which are displayed framed photographs of the various sites visited by the brothers during their recent travels in Italy. In 1895 they had been in Venice, revisiting it the following year, then travelling on to Padua, Bologna, Ferrara, Ravenna, Faenza and Florence.

At the lower left is to be seen an image of the Riva degli Schiavoni, where Sigmund and Alexander had stayed during their Venetian visit of 1895; above that are images of the Palace of Theoderic in Ravenna and of a weathercock. To the upper right of this last there hangs another view of Venice, showing the Grand Canal; and to the upper left of Freud's head is a photograph of one of the sarcophagi to be found in the Campo Santo in Bologna. This shows two children at the bedside of a third: a figural group forming part of the Monumento Minghetti. To the right of that image is one of a mother holding her child, from the Monumento Bersani. Displayed towards the window are photographs of putti from a relief by Donatello in the Museo del Duomo in Florence and, below that, a further framed image from Venice: in this case of the Piazza San Marco. Below that, and as if horizontally aligned with the image of the Palace of Theoderic, is a photograph of two of the famous towers in Bologna: the Torre Asinelli and the Torre Garisenda. A third image from Venice is here largely masked by Freud's head.[3]

1 Molnar 2007; Bergstein 2010, p. 43.
2 In am grateful to Christfried Tögel for this information.
3 The identification of the displayed images is owed to Molnar 2007, pp. 123–24.

The date inscribed below Alexander's photograph of his brother, 17th June 1897, is that of the fifteenth anniversary of Sigmund's engagement to Martha Bernays.[4] In surrounding Freud's head and upper body in the manner of a halo, these images may be seen to possess a programmatic character with a significance beyond their immediate role as mementoes of travel in Italy. The considerations that follow – on Freud's relationship with images and with collecting – here serve to investigate that further dimension.

The myth of a fixation on words

Sigmund Freud himself largely avoided including images within any form of self-definition; nor did he overtly approve of their incorporation within psychoanalytic practice. There accordingly still prevails the view that Freudian psychoanalysis was and is "nothing but an exchange of words".[5] It does, indeed, proceed by way of a form of conversation, and in that is to be found its strength, but also its limitation, for it is thereby above all fixated on two sensory organs: the mouth and the ear. Yet the invariably meticulous installation of a consulting room may also create the desired ambience through drawing directly upon the world of the visual, even if that aspect is in due course to be tamed or neutralised.[6] In the case of Freud, however, this visual aspect was eventually to comprise between 2,000 and 3,000 small sculpted figures, which he had acquired over many years and which were displayed virtually throughout his consulting room and the neighbouring study. In no sense could these be described as mere decoration for these spaces; rather, they were the outcome of Freud's positive obsession with collecting. This aspect of Freud's own practice was one that issued at length in his being characterised as "the great veiler" (*"der grosse Verhüller"*). But it also crucially assisted him as he sought to keep scientific enquiry free of a personal dimension and thereby to protect it.[7] The act of "veiling" may, in this case, be seen to belong within the honourable tradition of "honest deception" (*"dissimilazione onesta"*).[8]

The concern here to better understand Freud's status in this respect draws on a number of earlier attempts to re-examine the "myth of the prioritisation of the spoken word within the history of psychoanalysis".[9] Central to this enterprise, and to be considered first of all, is Freud's masterful examination of Michel-

4 Molnar 2007, p. 120.
5 *Freud, Berggasse 19* 2020, p. 194.
6 Ruhs 2006; Ruhs 2020, p. 205.
7 Cremerius 1971.
8 *Dissimulazione onesta oder Die ehrliche Verstellung* (2007).
9 Carroy 2009. In addition to the recognition of the haptic aspect of the book (Marinelli 2009), there has also been the matter of the couch (Marinelli 2006).

angelo's *Moses*, published in the Viennese journal *Imago* in the spring of 1914. Apart from his text of 1910 on Leonardo da Vinci, it was in particular his engagement with the monumental marble figure in the church of San Pietro in Vincoli in Rome that gave Freud the model for a psychoanalytic concern with historical biography and with the image.[10] The second focus of enquiry here will be Freud's collection of "idols" from Antiquity. Freud brought to the amassing of these a passion that he himself compared with his addiction to smoking.[11] This and his subsequent engagement with them reveal that they were for him far more than mere exhibits for display in a vitrine.

A new basis for research

A great deal of scholarly attention has been devoted to Freud's research into Michelangelo's *Moses*.[12] The items in his collection have also been the subject of both striking analysis and remarkable exhibitions;[13] and, in that context, it has repeatedly been observed that the small sculpted figures did not merely bear silent witness to Freud's analytical practice, but were, rather, actively incorporated within it.[14] But it is generally the case that Freud's study of the *Moses* and

10 Sigmund Freud, "Eine Kindheitserinnerung des Leonardo da Vinci", in: *SFG*, vol. 12, pp. 65–128; on this point see also: Herding 1998; Sigmund Freud, "Der Moses des Michelangelo", in *SFG*, vol. 14, pp. 19–45.

11 Letter of 7th February 1931 from Sigmund Freud to Stefan Zweig, in: Freud 1968, pp. 420–21; and see below, p. 74.

12 For a summary of the literature, see Grubrich-Simitis 2004. For the most recent comprehensive analysis, see Simmons 2006, pp. 214–64. Freud's "aesthetic" and his influence on the fine arts are addressed by Jack J. Spector (Spector 1972). My own text here concentrates on Freud's essay on the *Moses* of Michelangelo and on Freud's collection.

13 Heinz and Carina Weiss were the first to address the significance of Freud's collection "for his theoretical and practical work" through an analysis of individual pieces (Weiss & Weiss 1984, p. 213). Barely any attention has been paid to their work in this respect, even though their study was itself the fruitful outcome of an exemplary interplay of archaeology and psychoanalysis. Important stages in further research on the collection have been marked by: *Sigmund Freud and Art*, 1989; D'Agata 1994; *Excavations and Their Objects*, 1996; *"Meine . . . alten und dreckigen Götter*, 1998; *Freud's Sculpture*, 2006; Mayer 2001, pp. 189–90, 193–98; Montserrat 2001; Ucko 2011; Burke 2006; Müller 2019, pp. 172–317; O'Donoghue 2019, pp. 87–119. My own attempts at interpretation are closest to those of Diana Fuss in her endeavour to understand the interiors in question as resonant spaces equipped with sculpted figures (Fuss 2004, pp. 71–105, esp. 99–101). Cf. also *Freud's Antiquity*, 2023.

14 Lydia Marinelli started with the assumption that the items in Freud's collection "in many respects participated in the work of analysis" (Marinelli 1998, p. 11); and John Forrester came to the same conclusion: "Freud's collections were thus inseparably interconnected with his daily work of analysis" (Forrester 1998, p. 32). Andreas Mayer has written, in a similar

his activity as a collector are treated as if they were entirely separate aspects of his life. As a result, there has seemed to be little reason to consider and compare the methods he employed in each case.

Newly available sources offer, however, the opportunity to re-think both areas in relation to each other. Chief among these are Freud's notebooks, which in 2009 were discovered among the Sigmund Freud Papers at the Library of Congress in Washington, D. C. Since their publication, in 2021, these have constituted a new basis for research into numerous aspects of Freud's life, both private and public, as also into his work as a scientist.[15] It is above all the visits that Freud made to Rome in 1907 and in 1912 that, in the light of this rediscovered record of his observations and the insights they record, assume a heretofore unknown dimension.[16] An entirely new approach to the study of Freud has also been enabled through the steady publication, between 2105 and 2023, of the *Sigmund-Freud-Gesamtausgabe* (*SFG*), edited by Chistfried Tögel. Here, each item, most thoroughly contextualised, occupies its correct chronological position; numerous, previously unedited texts (for example, the early, so-called pre-analytic writings) are incorporated; and both lectures and interviews are included.[17]

My original intention had been to restrict my own reflections on Freud to a single chapter in the book on the work and life of Michelangelo that I published in 2021. It was, however, soon apparent that the sheer wealth of the material I had amassed was threatening to overwhelm the space reserved for it and thereby to undermine the cohesion of the volume as a whole. In the end I had scope for little more than a series of concise observations,[18] some of which have been absorbed into the present publication. At the invitation of Gottfried Boehm, I was able, in November 2021, to present further material at a lecture given under the auspices of the Jacob Burckhardt-Gespräche auf Castelen in Augst, near Basel. And the out-

sense, of "relations with objects" that, through their strongly tactile aspect, constituted an essential component of Freud's analytical technique (Mayer 2001, pp. 189–90, 193–98). And Diane O'Donoghue attributed to the sculpted figures the character of *agents provocateurs* (O'Donoghue 2019, pp. 5, 109). Pursuing a similar line of thought, Felix Jäger (Jäger 2023) arrives at complementary ideas, above all through the incorporation of materials from the psychology of suggestion and contemporary museum displays. The 2023 London exhibition *Freud's Antiquity* similarly emphasises the role of Freud's collection for the methods he employed in psychoanalysis.

15 Freud 2021. The material was discovered by Gerhard Fichtner, Albrecht Hirschmüller and Christfried Tögel. On the history of the discovery and on the publication: Hirschmüller & Tögel 2021.

16 D'Angelo 2020, pp. 205–20, 263–82.

17 All works by Freud mentioned in what follows are cited in this edition (*SFG*, vols. 1–23, 2015–2023).

18 Bredekamp 2021a, pp. 299–303.

come of further investigations has been added to the extended version of that lecture in its present, printed form.[19]

My engagement with this subject ultimately derives from the impulse sparked by two particular encounters. The more recent of these involved a series of conversations with the historian Peter Paret, in the academic year 1991 / 92 at the Institute of Advanced Study in Princeton. I was particularly struck by the extent to which the history of Paret's own family (he had been born in Berlin in 1924) featured in what he was able to recall and confide. Peter Paret was the son of the philosopher and art historian Hans Paret and the psychoanalyst Suzanne (Suse) Aimée Cassirer. She was herself the daughter of Paul Cassirer, the celebrated gallerist and publisher to modernist and avant-garde Berlin from the 1890s to the 1920s. Before Suzanne Cassirer had transferred her chief interest to medicine and psychoanalysis, she had studied art history and philosophy in Marburg, and philosophy with Ernst Cassirer in Hamburg. In 1932–33 she underwent a course of psychoanalysis with Sigmund Freud, as part of her training. A further such course, with Siegfried Bernfeld (the first psychoanalyst to seek to establish a connection between Freud and Marx), led to an affair, and in due course Suzanne's divorce from Hans Paret. Peter Paret remained with his mother. After emigrating to the USA, Suzanne and Siegfried were able to compile and in due course publish a great deal of information on Freud, including source material that continues to be of assistance to researchers.[20] In 1951 Suzanne Cassirer Bernfeld published the first account of Freud's collection and its role both in his life and in his practice as a psychoanalyst.[21] My conversations with Peter Paret may thus be said to have served as the point of origin for my desire to revisit the earlier scholarship and to make an attempt at reconstructing what I have here termed Freud's figural psychoanalysis.

The second of the two encounters took place at one of several lectures given by Gustav Ernst Störring, Director of the Clinic for Psychiatry and Nervous Diseases at the University of Kiel.[22] Before Störring's retirement, in 1968, I was able, during my first semester as a university student, to attend one such event. Accompanied by his patient, and with her consent, he carried out demonstrations of his analytical procedure before an audience gathered in the lecture hall. During the course of this, he resorted also to visual means. His approach to the treatment of this woman, who suffered from an acute fear of knives, was unforgettable. He induced her to watch the crucial scenes in Alfred Hitchcock's *Psycho* in order, by

19 Bredekamp 2006; Bredekamp 2022.

20 Bernfeld & Cassirer Bernfeld 1988.

21 Cassirer Bernfeld 1951.

22 Völkel 2000.

way of the acute disturbance triggered by this experience, to penetrate into the sources of her violent fantasies. Nowadays, such an occurrence would probably no longer be permitted. But its impact upon me was such that it has remained with me ever since. And I have repeatedly been moved to return to the question as to whether there could indeed be such an entity as a Freudian visual psychoanalysis. In that sense, the present book may also be viewed as an acknowledgement of that lecture in Kiel.

Like the text of almost all the books I have published, that of this one, too, was written on the Rehmstackerdeich in Eiderstedt. I dedicate it to those images that intermittently emerge, like faces glimpsed in a dream, from the mist that hovers over the surrounding fens.

I FREUD'S ANALYSIS OF MICHELANGELO'S *MOSES*

1. Freud the traveller

Travel, archaeology, psychoanalysis

Travel, for Freud, in particular his visits to Rome and to other Italian cities, offered not only a great many occasions for the acquisition of further knowledge and the chance to indulge in living well, but also, and above all, an opportunity to gaze into the mirror of the self, in which every imaginable mood and thought might find a reflection. When in Italy, he initially took delight in the beauty of the landscape, of the cities and of the people, qualities that he would rediscover in works of art. The immense happiness generated in him through the pleasure brought by these experiences was, however, also liable to leave him thereafter feeling oppressed and isolated.[1] As Freud was later to record, he felt his own relationship with the city of Rome to be "deeply neurotic".[2] This relationship was embodied in the contradiction between two of Freud's idols: Hannibal, that city's enemy, and Johann Joachim Winckelmann, its worshipper.[3] Freud sensed in Rome so powerful a challenge to his own psyche that he put off visiting it until he felt he had become sufficiently resilient through completing a course of self-analysis.

A reflection of Freud's scientific methods was already directly incorporated within the personal dimension of his experience of travel, for he recognised that the aims and means of psychoanalysis and those of archaeology were effectively

1 From the literature on Freud's travels: Tögel 2003; Schlesier 2004; Kogel 2019; D'Angelo 2020.

2 Letter of 3rd December 1897 from Sigmund Freud to Wilhelm Fliess, in Freud 1950, p. 251.

3 Cf. Schorske 1980, p. 191–93; Zapperi 2013, pp. 206–07 (on Hannibal); Biemann 2016, pp. 61–65; Müller 2019, pp. 178–80.

one and the same.[4] He developed this notion in a lecture given in May 1896, to members of the Verein für Psychiatrie und Neurologie in Vienna: "On the Aetiology of Hysteria".

Freud imagined an archaeologist who, in an all but unexplored region, comes upon an expanse of ruins. He takes notes on those that are visible, enquires among the local inhabitants as to what they know of the site, and then continues on his way. An alternative approach is then offered in an account of archaeological exploration that is clearly intended as an allegory of psychoanalysis:

> "He [the archaeologist] might proceed in another fashion; he might have brought with him picks, shovels and spades, he might have encouraged the locals to wield these tools and, in company with them, he might have been able to take the site in hand, to clear away the rubble, and to render visible those remains that had formerly been buried. If the work proved successful, this would be apparent in the very nature of the discoveries that followed: that the ruined walls were a fragment of those that once surrounded a palace or a treasure-house, that the ruined columns attested to the former presence of a temple, and that the numerous discarded, and fortunately bi-lingual, inscriptions revealed an alphabet and a language, the deciphering and translation of which would yield undreamt-of insights into events in the remote past, in memory of which these monuments had been erected. *Saxa loquuntur*!"[5]

It was above all during his visits to Rome that Freud was able to explore this analogy, almost as if through his own feet and hands. This experience was, without doubt, one of the motivating factors in his decision to start collecting small, sculpted figures from Antiquity: items that attentive excavation had claimed back from the earth. In doing so, Freud was able to assert a stronger hold upon the portable and material products of excavation, in which he saw a synonym for his own activity as a psychoanalyst. The Latin phrase "*Saxa loquuntur*" (the stones speak), used at the end of the quoted passage, may here also be understood as a motto both for Freud's own collection and for his preoccupation with Michelangelo's *Moses*.

4 From the wealth of literature on this subject: Cassirer Bernfeld 1951; Kuspit 1989; Handler Spitz 1989; Stockreiter 1998; Tögel 1989, pp. 13–16; Stephan 2011.

5 Sigmund Freud, "Zur Aetiologie der Hysterie", in: *SFG*, vol. 5, pp. 471–501, here 474. Cf. Tôgel 1989, pp. 13–16.

The *Moses*

Freud's first confrontation with the marble figure that occupies the centre of the lower level of the tomb of Pope Julius II in the church of San Pietro in Vincoli in Rome (Fig. 2) had upon him one of the strongest impressions he was to receive in his entire life. During every one of his longer visits to Rome – the first of these in September 1901 and the last, in the company of his daughter Anna, in September 1923 – he made a point of seeking out the *Moses*.[6]

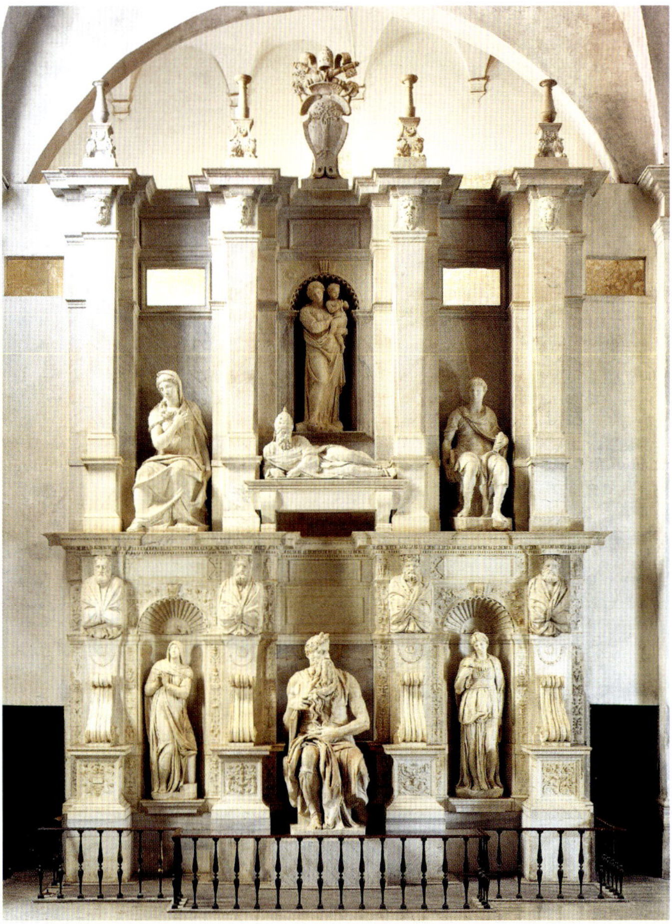

2| Michelangelo, The Tomb of Pope Julius II, 1542. Marble. Rome, San Pietro in Vincoli

6 *Sigmund Freud* 2003, p. 380.

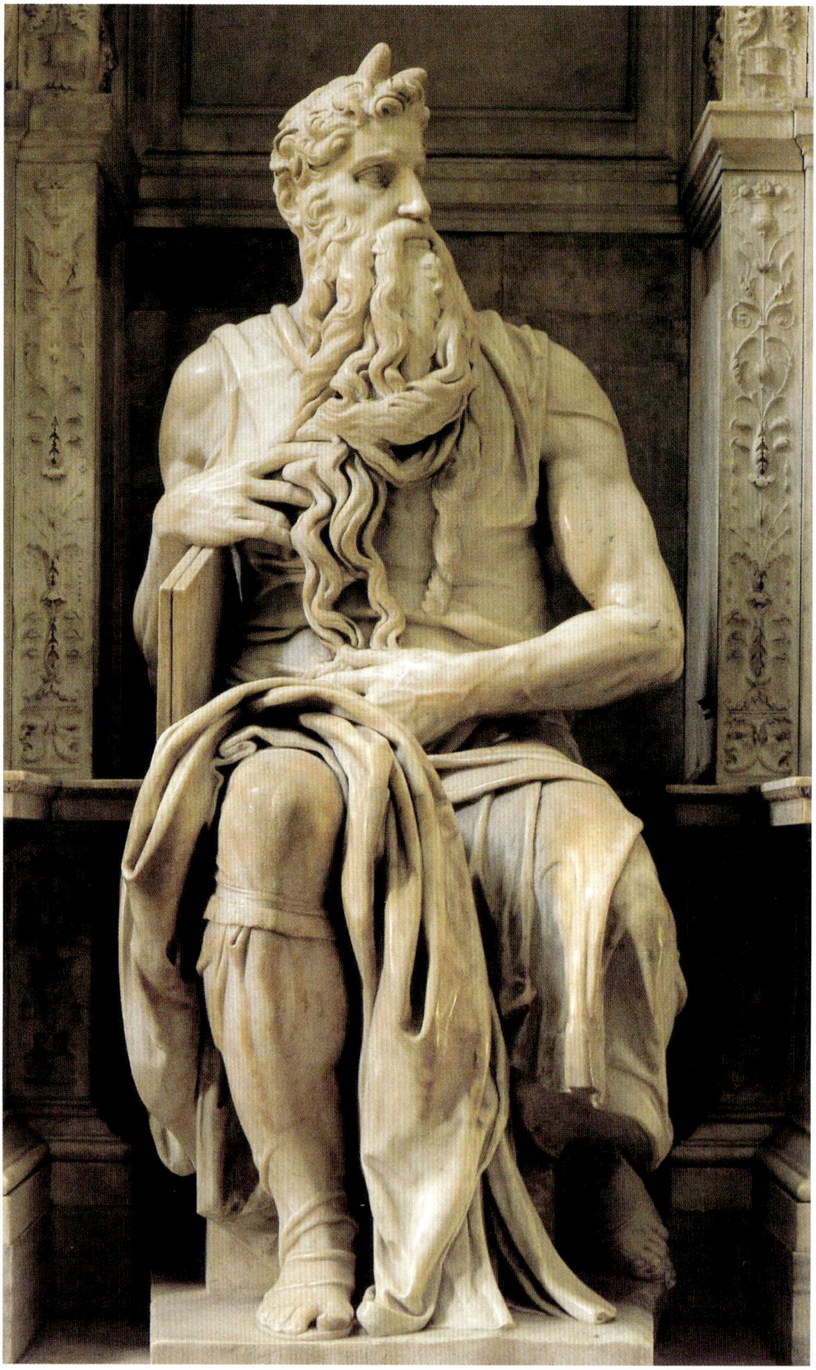

3| Michelangelo, *Moses* (forming part of the Tomb of Pope Julius II), 1513–15. Marble. Rome, San Pietro in Vincoli

When Freud first encountered Michelangelo's figure this was no longer located as had originally been intended. Produced in the years 1513 / 14, it was to have been placed on the upper level of the tomb, which was due to be installed in the new St. Peter's. Positioned thus, it would have struck the observer as visually accessible from several sides.[7] In 1542, however, when the tomb was reworked prior to its re-erection in the church where it thereafter remained, the *Moses* was allotted a position at the centre of its lower level. As recorded in the engraving made in 1554 by Antonio Salamanca, Michelangelo had now drawn the figure deep into its niche, as if wishing, through the resulting sense of compression, to reinforce as far as possible the contradiction between emotional eruption and unbending self-control.[8] To the sensibility of the Enlightenment, however, with its enthusiasm for space and air, such an arrangement was simply intolerable. In 1818, on the initiative of the sculptor Antonio Canova, among others, the *Moses* was temporarily extracted from its niche in order to be placed upon a higher pedestal.[9] The seated figure as Freud came to know it, in its 19th-century installation – which imparted to it a greater degree of freedom – was, in several respects, closer to how it would originally have appeared.

In the essay on Michelangelo's *Moses* that Freud published in 1914 he left his readers in no doubt as to the status of this marble figure. His confession to never having "experienced so strong an effect in the case of any other work of sculpture"[10] would appear to allow no room for subtleties of interpretation. But the following passage draws attention to Freud's awareness of the simultaneous attraction and repulsion exerted by this work:

> "How often have I climbed the steep steps from the unlovely Corso Cavour to the piazza where the deserted church stands, always seeking to resist the contemptuous, angry stare of the hero, and sometimes I have then gingerly crept out of the half-darkness of the interior as if I myself belonged among that rabble upon which his eye was fixed".[11]

In Freud's emphasis on his own movements – his climbing up to the piazza, his confrontation with the figure of *Moses*, the final act of creeping gingerly out of the church – one can sense what a mental tumult must have been stirred in the head of the father of psychoanalysis whenever he looked upon the *Moses* (Fig. 3). His

7 Bredekamp 2021a, p. 182–83, and fig. 1 on p. 276.
8 Bredekamp 2021a, p. 579.
9 Frommel 2014, p. 352; fig. 33 on p. 297.
10 *Sigmund Freud* 2003, p. 380.
11 Sigmund Freud, "Der Moses des Michelangelo", in: *SFG*, vol. 14, p. 23.

perceptions veer between a focus on self-identification and an attempt to achieve distance. As he is torn between enticement and aversion, Freud's sense of himself gives rise to a perception of his own role in the establishment of psychoanalysis.

A chance meeting: 1901

The first journey to Rome that Freud made in the company of his brother Alexander, during the first two weeks of September 1901, appeared to him as "a high point in life".[12] On this occasion, however, the *Moses* was not among the sights that he directly sought out. On the fourth day of their stay, 6th September, he reported to his wife, Martha, that, after visiting the Pantheon, he had "then suddenly seen the *Moses* of Michelangelo in the church of San Pietro in Vincoli", albeit without having intended to do so. This encounter had come about, rather, as he added in explanation, "suddenly, through a misunderstanding".[13] One may assume that Freud had lost his way and had unexpectedly come across the church with Michelangelo's figure. However unplanned the encounter may have been, its impact on Freud could hardly have been more profound. It was evidently this event that prompted his observation: "this afternoon impressions on which we'll live for years".[14]

This statement was no exaggeration, even if Freud would not go to see the *Moses* when in Italy a year later, towards the end of August 1902.[15] Rome, on that occasion, was merely a stop on the way to Naples and the excavations once again underway at Pompeii, which were to become for Freud another crucial experience.[16]

The programmatic photograph: 1906

A photographic portrait of Sigmund Freud that is no less eloquent than that produced by his brother Alexander (see Fig. 1) attests to his affinity with the work of Michelangelo. This later shot (Fig. 4) was taken by Freud's eldest son, Martin: it shows the boy's father seated on the veranda that adjoined the room he used as

12 Letter of 19th September 1901 from Sigmund Freud to Wilhelm Fliess, in: Freud / Fliess 1986, p. 493.

13 Letter of 6th September 1901 from Sigmund Freud to Wilhelm Fliess, in: *Sigmund Freud* 2003, p. 142.

14 Letter of 6th September 1901 from Sigmund Freud to Martha Freud, in *Sigmund Freud* 2003, p. 142.

15 Letter of 30th August 1902 from Sigmund Freud to Martha Freud, in: *Sigmund Freud* 2003, pp. 154–55.

16 D'Angelo 2020, p. 162–71.

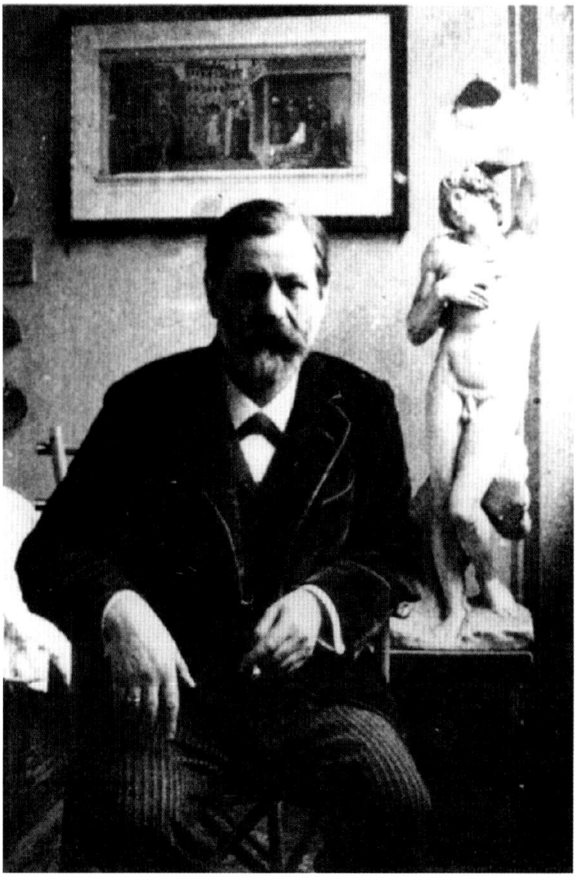

4| Martin Freud, Portrait of Sigmund Freud, December 1906. Photograph. London, Freud Museum

his study when the family apartment was still on the ground floor at 19 Berggasse.[17] Freud's decision that they should move to the first floor may well have prompted the taking of this photograph.[18]

Here, Freud is seated on a chair and looking directly into the camera. The upper part of his head crops the base of a framed image on the wall behind: a

17 The inscription reads: "Mein erster Schnappschuss von Vater in seinem Arbeitszimmer" [My first snapshot of father in his study] (Freud, Martin 1999, p. 38. Cf. *Sigmund Freud* 1985, no. 217, p. 201; D'Angelo 2020, p. 65).

18 Gamwell 1989, p. 31, note 26, discusses a variety of further datings between 1905 (her own) and 1914. The move to the first floor took place not, as reported by Ernest Jones (Jones 1955, p. 424), in spring 1908, but in December 1906 (I am grateful to Christfried Tögel for this information).

reproduction of the fresco by Masolino and Masaccio in the Brancacci Chapel in Florence that shows Saint Peter healing a disabled man and Tabitha, a young disciple of Jesus, being restored to life. Without doubt, there is here more than a hint at a connection with the capacities of a medical man who, like Peter, is able to "perform miracles".[19]

The sculpted figure seen to the right and slightly to the rear of the seated subject, is a plaster cast of Michelangelo's *Dying Prisoner.*[20] It is probable that Freud acquired this, along with other casts, in Florence in September 1896. He wrote of such purchases to Wilhelm Fliess, his fatherly friend and partner in self-diagnosis: "I have now decorated my room with casts of Florentine statues".[21] Freud doubtless saw in the *Dying Prisoner* both a token of the Florence of Michelangelo and a souvenir of his own, earlier visits to the Louvre, where the original was to be found.[22]

In its subtle exposition of transitions between waking and sleeping, life and death, embodied in an image that commentators have invariably found to be highly erotic, the sculpted figure might well serve here as the genius of the psychoanalyst. Like Michelangelo's *Moses*, the *Dying Prisoner* was made for incorporation within the tomb of Julius II.[23] It seems, then, as if Freud has here expressly posed alongside the plaster cast of this work in order to re-enact, through his own person, the originally intended figural interrelationship,[24] albeit without assuming an air of the inner tension that is so integral to the *Moses*. Freud's right hand does not delve into his beard but has the tips of its extended fingers resting on his thigh, and his left is not pressed against his stomach but holds the obligatory cigar.

19 Bergstein 2010, p. 49.

20 Bredekamp 2021a, pp. 284–93.

21 Letter of 6th December 1896 from Sigmund Freud to Wilhelm Fliess, in Freud / Fliess 1986, p. 226. On Freud's living arrangements at this time, see Freud / Fliess 1986, p. 140. On Freud's friendship with Fliess: Tögel 2006, pp. 31–37.

22 Letter of 19th October 1885 from Sigmund Freud to Martha Bernays, in Freud 1968, p. 177; also 191.

23 Bredekamp 2021a, pp. 284–93.

24 On alternative interpretations, which see in the presence here of the *Dying Prisoner* an allusion to the death of Freud's father, cf. D'Angelo 2020, pp. 65–67.

Depression: 1907

During the next year, 1907, the traces of such a sense of connection and, with them, Freud's extremely high spirits, had deserted him. The Mittwochgesellschaft (Wednesday Society), established in 1902, a circle of those with a strong interest in Freudian psychoanalysis, had so lost its cohesion that Freud, overcome by despair, had dissolved it. This development cast its shadow over the journey to Italy on which he embarked in September of that year, in the company of his sister-in-law, Minna. The latter, moreover, when they had reached Florence, received news of the death of a friend and resolved to return to Vienna, leaving Freud to continue further south on his own.[25]

The feelings of failure and loneliness that had overcome Freud in his work as a psychoanalyst now infected the entirety of this stay in Rome. The happiness that, in September 1901, had marked his first visit to the Eternal City, that symbol of splendour and prestige, now gave way to perplexity and melancholy. On 18th September he embarked on visits to the Forum and to Michelangelo's *Moses* in San Pietro in Vincoli.[26] In a letter of that date to his family there is no mention of an encounter with the marble figure;[27] in his notebook, however, Freud did remark: "Extraordinary how much despotism or subjectivity there is in every [artistic] representation, and how grateful we must be for this accessory".[28] One would be inclined to assume that this entry related directly to the *Moses*; but the explanatory bracketed words – "(Boni Forum Romanorum)" – suggest, rather, that Freud here also had in mind the excavations then underway in the Forum, as well as the archaeologist, Giacomo Boni, who was directing them. The note that follows does, however, relate solely to the *Moses*: "What can have moved Michelangelo to depict Moses as a River God? Even the travertine cascades in the manner of a waterfall".[29]

One may assume that this interpretation of the *Moses* as the representation of a River God had been prompted by the sight of the figural embodiments of the *Nile* and the *Tiber* that were to be found in the Piazza del Campidoglio. It is possible that Freud, in the course of viewing the Forum, had climbed up to the Capitol in order there to look at these reclining figures carved in travertine, or that he still

25 D'Angelo 2020, pp. 207–08.

26 Freud's notebook no.7, fol. 7.17, in: Freud 2021, p. 124.

27 Letter of 18th September 1907 from Sigmund Freud to his family, in: *Sigmund Freud* 2003, p. 217.

28 Freud's notebook no. 7, fol. 7.20, in: Freud 2021, p. 125.

29 Freud's notebook no. 7, fol. 7.21, in: Freud 2021, p. 125.

retained a visual memory of them from his first visit to Rome.[30] The beard hair of both the *Nile* and the *Tiber*, and in particular that of the former (Fig. 5), may well have suggested the notion of a waterfall, which Freud then rediscovered, in a more emphatic form, in the marble beard of Michelangelo's *Moses* (see Figs. 3, 13).

This was the first time that Freud had commented upon that beard, which was in due course to assume a central importance in his engagement with Michelangelo's figure. At this point he associated the aquatic aspect of the beard with that spring which Moses, through striking a rock, would cause to gush forth, to the relief of his thirsting people (*Numbers*: 20, 11).[31] Although the seemingly random associations made here were in fact quite promising, Freud did not pursue them.

Over the following days Freud was tormented with perpetual mood swings. On 20th September he noted: "I've now reduced my expectations by comparison with the plans I had when I arrived".[32] The next day, however, he felt more confidence in in his own abilities,[33] somewhat curiously linking them with a desire to be introduced by the archaeologist Giacomo Boni to the latest excavations being carried out in the Forum,[34] albeit concluding: "but nobody knows me here, I belong to the *misera plebs contribuens* [the impoverished tax-paying masses]".[35] On 23th September Freud captured his abiding sense of an encroaching darkness in the words: "The chief outcome of the stay in Rome is that I now see myself as very small, and everything of my own as meaningless".[36] Two days later, on the day of his departure, he added to his notebook the following words: "The acme of freedom: to be in Rome today and to have had enough of Rome".[37]

During the month of September 1907 Freud debated with himself his choice of career, his comrades-in-arms and, above all, the city of Rome as the mirror of his intellectual life; and Michelangelo's figure of *Moses* itself played a part in this.

30 The probability that Freud was here drawing on his own memories is supported by the fact that, in his notebook, he mentions the visit to the Capitol on 23th September 1907 (Freud's notebook no. 7, fol. 7.30, in Freud 2021, p. 127), but not that occurring on 19th September, that being the first day of his stay in Rome, a day on which he visited the Forum and Michelangelo's *Moses*.

31 Freud's notebook no. 7, fol. 7.21, in: Freud 2021, p. 125.

32 Freud's notebook no. 7, fol. 7.23, in: Freud 2021, p. 126.

33 Freud's notebook no. 7, fol. 7.24, in: Freud 2021, p. 126.

34 Freud's notebook no. 7, fol. 6.11r, in: D'Angelo 2020, pp. 302–03.

35 Freud's notebook no. 7, fol. 7.26, in: Freud 2021, pp. 126–27. The reference here (p. 127) to the origin of this dictum in Horace (*Sat.* 1.8.10) is incorrect. Nor is it to be found (as claimed in Rothauer 1895, p. 99) in the writings of the Hungarian constitutional lawyer István Werbőczi (1517).

36 Freud's notebook no. 7, fol. 7.34, in: Freud 2021, p. 129.

37 Freud's notebook no. 7, fol. 7.40, in: Freud 2021, p. 131.

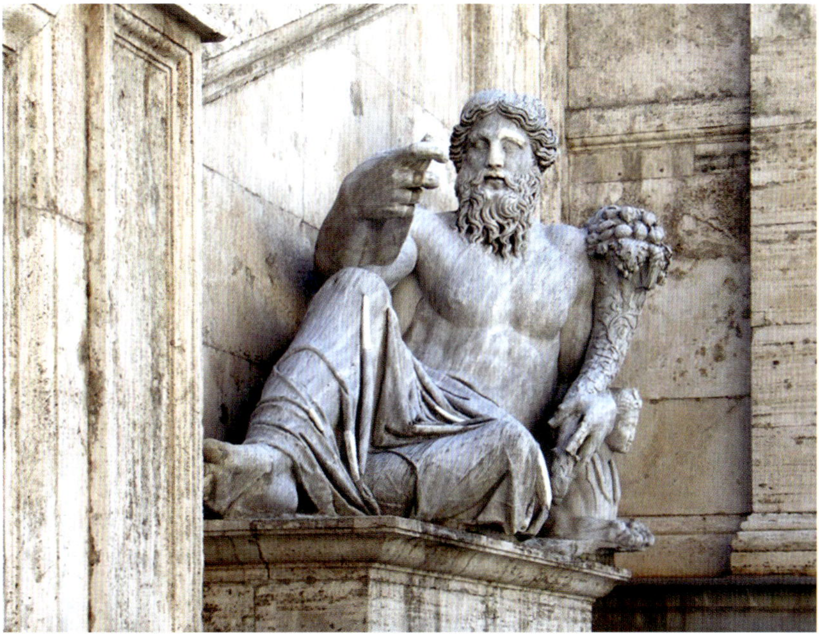

5| Anonymous, *The Nile*, 2nd century AD. Marble. Rome, Piazza del Campidoglio

Freud was at this time, in a certain sense, seeking to free himself of psychoanalysis. To Carl Gustav Jung, the psychoanalyst born in Basel, in whose work in Zürich Freud placed great and as yet unclouded hope, he confided on 19th September: "At the start of the vacation I buried scientific endeavour deep in the earth; I would like now to attend to myself and, once again, to really make something of myself".[38] While an exceptional figure such as Michelangelo's marble *Moses* usually challenged Freud to exert his emotional and intellectual powers, as of September 1907 Freud had neither the will nor the means to draw upon these. He seems, for a while, to have devoted no further serious thought to the *Moses*.

Identification with the biblical Moses: 1909

At the start of 1909, by which date international regard for psychoanalysis had grown, Freud took to comparing himself, in an entirely different frame of mind, with another Moses: that encountered in the Bible. On 17th January of that year he told C. G. Jung (who, born in 1875, was a generation younger than himself): "If I

38 Letter of 19th September 1907 from Sigmund Freud to C. G. Jung, in: Freud / Jung 1974, p. 98; cf. *Sigmund Freud* 2003, p. 217, note 19.

am Moses, then you will be Joshua, destined to occupy the Promised Land of Psychiatry, which I may behold only from afar".[39]

With this remark, Freud was alluding to the tragic circumstance that, after the Exodus from Egypt, Moses would lead the Israelites as far as the banks of the River Jordan, only to die before its crossing could be accomplished. Freud could thus hardly have bestowed a greater form of praise upon Jung than to declare that the scientific journey he had himself initiated, as Moses, should be taken to its intended destination by Jung, who would assume the role of Joshua. Michelangelo's *Moses* as yet played no role in this historical scheme, although a few years later the situation would alter dramatically.

The return of the "magic" of Rome: 1910

In September 1910 Freud, in the company of his pupil and friend, the Budapest-based Sándor Ferenczi (who was himself to become an important psychoanalyst), embarked on a journey to Sicily.[40] As in 1902, Rome on this occasion was largely to be a mere through-station as they journeyed further south. The few hours available to them for visiting sites in Rome were devoted entirely to the Forum, that archetype of the comparison between archaeology and psychoanalysis. On 6th September Freud wrote to his wife that he and Ferenczi had "spent two whole hours clambering about among the ruins, which in itself would have made the journey here worthwhile".[41] Nonetheless, on 7th September, he reported to her that "Rome, yet again, has been magical".[42]

39 Letter of 17th January 1909 from Sigmund Freud to C. G. Jung, in: Freud / Jung 1974, p. 218; cf. Grubrich-Simitis 2004, p. 16.

40 Kogel 2019, pp. 49–56. On the later complications following Ferenczi's relationship with his patient Elma Pálos: Jensen 2019, pp. 241–50.

41 Letter of 6th September 1910 from Sigmund Freud to Martha Freud, in: *Sigmund Freud* 2003, p. 340.

42 Letter of 7th September 1910 from Sigmund Freud to Martha Freud, in: *Sigmund Freud* 2003, p. 341.

2. Freud's text

The right hand of the *Moses*: 1912

The newly stirred high spirits were to be even higher during Freud's fifth visit to Rome, which he made between 16th and 29th September 1912, once again in the company of Sándor Ferenczi. Very shortly after their arrival and their installation in the Hotel Eden, from which they had a view across much of the city, Freud reported to his family: "The goal of living in Rome in the manner of a *grand seigneur* appears to have been realised!"[43] And on 20th September he wrote to his wife: "Rome has certainly been for me at its best. I'm enjoying it as never before, probably also because I'm living so splendidly".[44]

This enthusiasm found a reflection in Freud's engagement with the *Moses*. As he told his wife, he repeatedly went to see Michelangelo's figure: "I take pleasure in the exquisite, somewhat melancholic loneliness, then go out into the glorious weather and walk about a lot, up on the Palatine among the ruins, in the [gardens of the] Villa Borghese, a vast park, but utterly Roman in character, and I make a daily visit to the Michelangelo in S. Pietro in Vincoli".[45] The here added phrase "on which I'll, perhaps, write a few words" reveals that, at this point, Freud also felt ready to address the figure in a scholarly text.

Freud's intensive study of Michelangelo's figure is documented in a number of concise entries on a total of 14 pages of his notebook, by way of which he encapsulated the chief considerations to be addressed in the text he was to write the following year.[46] These focus on the implicit prior movements of the right hand and on the positioning and appearance of the two Tablets of the Law (Fig. 6).[47]

The notes aim at encouraging a view of the depicted moment as the endpoint of a succession of those that would have preceded it: "3 fingers outside the beard, only [no.] 2 pressing upon it [.] The hand has slipped down from where it was".[48] Freud made a small sketch (Fig. 7) in order to explain that, as a result of the pulling away of the hand, two locks of hair had intruded between the thumb and the forefinger lying upon them, while the ends of the remaining three fingers were

43 Letter of 16th September 1912 from Sigmund Freud to his family, in: *Sigmund Freud* 2003, p. 365.

44 Letter of 20th September 1912 from Sigmund Freud to Martha Freud, in: *Sigmund Freud* 2003, p. 368.

45 Letter of 25th September 1912 from Sigmund Freud to Martha Freud, in *Sigmund Freud* 2003, p. 370.

46 Freud's notebook no. 10, fols. 10.90–10.104, in: Freud 2012, pp. 241–44.

47 Bredekamp 2021a, p. 304, fig. 44.

48 Freud's notebook no. 10, fol. 10.91, in: Freud 2021, p. 241.

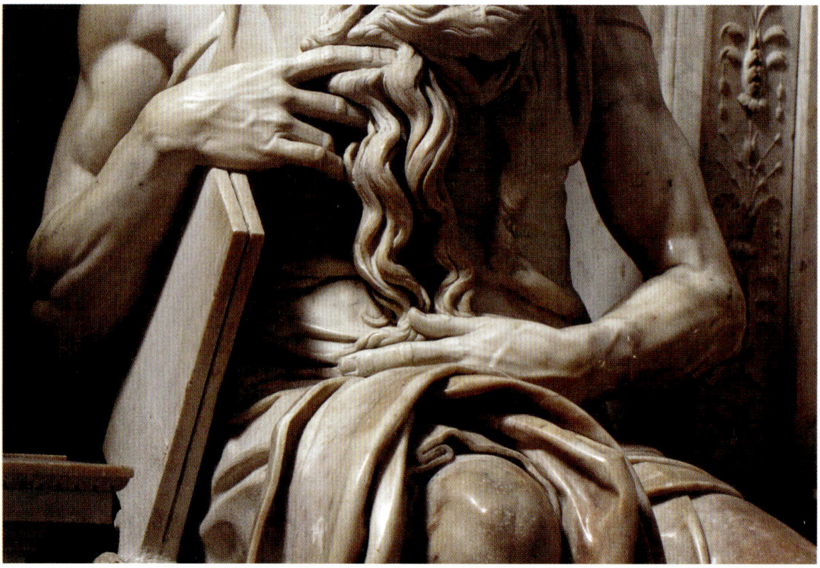

6| Michelangelo, *Moses*: torso, arms, hands, beard, Tablets of the Law. 1513–15. Marble. Rome, San Pietro in Vincoli

covered by these strands. The right hand as depicted is, accordingly, the outcome of a shift in its own position, and it can thereby be said to equate to one of the "remains of vehement impulses" triggered by a turn of the head to the figure's left.[49]

In another sketch (Fig. 8), Freud registers the fact that the Tablets of the Law are being held in place only by the edge of the palm and "the edge of the little finger".[50] He assumes that the Tablets would initially have been held, supported by the right arm and hand, in an upright position, forming a vertical line from the figure's hip to its armpit. When the right hand had suddenly moved to clasp the beard, the Tablets would have seemed as if about to fall. In response, Moses would have drawn his right arm back, while "the [right] hand would have caught hold of [what was now] the upper corner". The narrowly avoided "fall of the Tablets warned of the urgent need for [such a] change".[51]

The following entries were the product of a very precise way of looking at the Tablets themselves. At their lower edge Freud noticed a spur, which he made a point of recording in a separate drawing (Fig. 9).[52] As this spur would have been

49 Freud's notebook no. 10, fol. 10.92, in: Freud 2021, p. 242.
50 Freud's notebook no. 10, fol. 10.93, in: Freud 2021, p. 242.
51 Freud's notebook no. 10, fols. 10.94–10.95, in: Freud 2012, p. 242.
52 Freud's notebook no. 10, fol. 10.96, in: Freud 2012, p. 242.

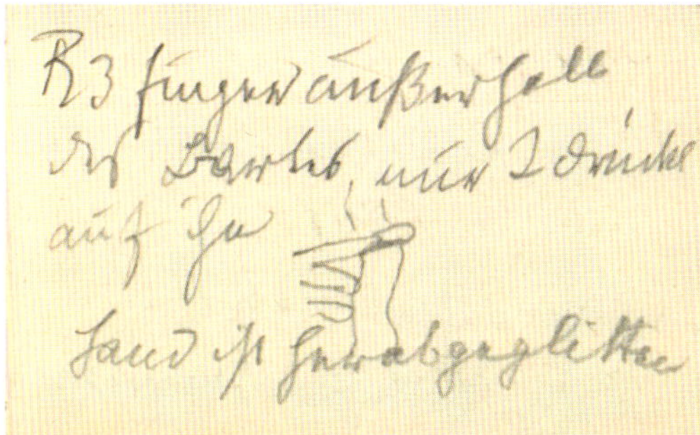

7| Sigmund Freud, Sketch of the fingers of the right hand of Michelangelo's *Moses*. Notebook no. 10, fol. 10.91. Sigmund Freud Papers, Library of Congress, Washington, D. C.

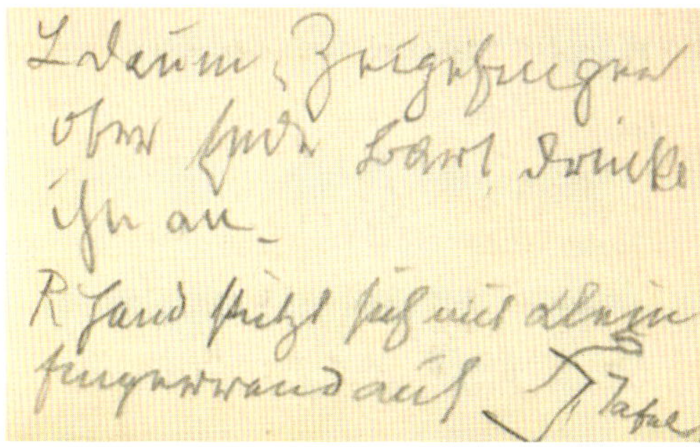

8| Sigmund Freud, Sketch of the Tablets of the Law held by Michelangelo's *Moses*. Notebook no. 10, fol. 10.93. Sigmund Freud Papers, Library of Congress, Washington, D. C.

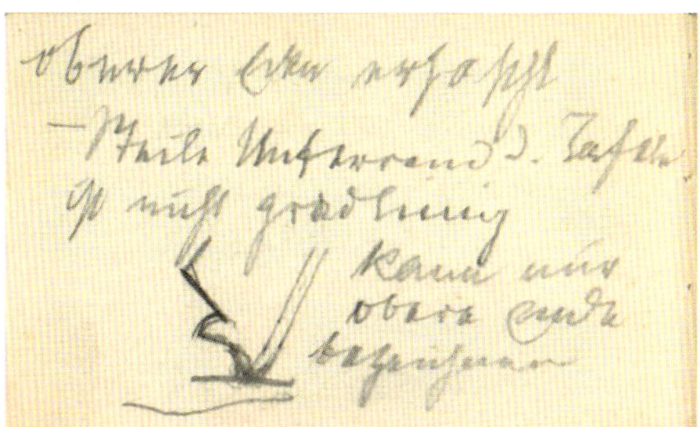

9| Sigmund Freud, Sketch of the spur on the Tablets of the Law held by Michelangelo's *Moses*. Notebook no. 10, fol. 10.96. Sigmund Freud Papers, Library of Congress, Washington, D. C.

added as a form of decoration only towards the upper edge (where it might originally have served the right hand as a support), this meant that it was clear that the Tablets as now depicted were in fact upside down. This made it all the more necessary that they be pressed against each other in order to protect them from falling and breaking.[53]

53 Freud's notebook no. 10, fols. 10.96–10.97, in: Freud 2021, p. 242; and fols. 10.102–10.104, in: Freud 2021, p. 244. These entries contradict Gerd Blum's suggestion that a derogatory gesture might have been implicit in the act of turning the Tablets of the Law upside down (Blum 2020, pp. 51–52, 58).

With the greatest possible subtlety, Freud has here contrived a theatre of gestures out of the positioning of the Tablets and the imagined movements of the fingers of the right hand that would have been triggered by a sudden turn of the head. Freud's analysis of the "remains of vehement impulses" is to be understood as an analysis of form that, regardless of the depicted object, incorporates the movements that have given rise to it. By this means he arrived at a view of the sculpted figure that was comparable to a psychic state, such as those that he, in his own psychoanalytic practice, sought to excavate in his search for traces of emotion. And here the impulse lay within Freud himself. In these first descriptions of the figure, written in September 1912, it becomes clear that this had, for him, become a touchstone for the psychoanalytical method as a means of delving beneath the masks of psychic problems, to lay bare the dynamic of the underlying histories of conflict and trauma. Hence Freud's acute enthusiasm regarding this particular work of sculpture; and this in turn drove him to make further studies of it and then, finally, to prepare an article on it.

The trauma of the schism

It was during this phase in Freud's research into the *Moses* that difficulties in his relationship with C. G. Jung, which had already grown somewhat troubled, came to a head. Jung had evolved an extended concept of the libido that could not be reconciled with Freud's notion of the interconnection between sexuality and other instinctual drives. Freud, for his part, was so rigorous in his rejection of this alternative to his own views and methods that he was even moved to compare it with the apostasy of the Israelites. In October 1912, not long after returning from the journey to Rome that he had made with Ferenczi, Freud told the latter: "As regards the atmosphere generated by a personality, I see myself as closer to the historic Moses than to Moses as interpreted by Michelangelo".[54]

The difference of views between Freud and Jung illustrates to what extent Freud's research into Michelangelo's *Moses* was marked by the troubling schism in the psychoanalytic movement, which indeed impacted the lives of all its members. Freud's differentiation between the Moses of the Old Testament and that of Michelangelo's marble figure was related to the difference between two distinct reactions to the apostasy of the Israelites. According to the biblical account, while Moses had ascended Mount Sinai in order there to receive the Tablets of the Law inscribed with the Ten Commandments, the Israelites had taken to worshipping

54 Letter of 17th October 1912 from Sigmund Freud to Sándor Ferenczi, in: Freud / Ferenczi 1993, p. 132. Cf. Simmons 2006, pp. 216–17. On the conflict with C. G. Jung: Whitebook 2020, pp. 273–77; Schröter 2023, pp. 160–64.

a Golden Calf. In response to this outrage, Moses had instigated ferocious retaliation (*Exodus*: 32, 28). When Freud, in a letter to Ferenczi, alluded to this episode, Ferenczi suggested that Jung himself would surely provoke in Freud much the same rage as Moses had brought to punishing the apostate Israelites.

In this situation the analysis of the marble *Moses* became an oracle for Freud's own self-examination as to whether his reaction to the conflict with Jung was appropriate or, indeed, in keeping with his own position in the psychoanalytic movement. If Freud's rage at the apostasy of Jung, whom he had once implicitly appointed his successor, was akin to that of the Moses of the Old Testament, it was through the examination of Michelangelo's *Moses* that he was able to seek, if not eventually himself to pursue, alternatives.

Further studies of the Tablets of the Law

During the weeks after his return from Rome, Freud set about familiarising himself with the most relevant scholarly literature, among which he particularly came to value the work of the English writer William Watkiss Lloyd.[55] As he told Ferenczi, in a letter of 27th October, he was also seeking to further inform his considerations through making visits to the collection of plaster casts, including one of Michelangelo's *Moses*, at the Viennese Akademie der bildenden Künste

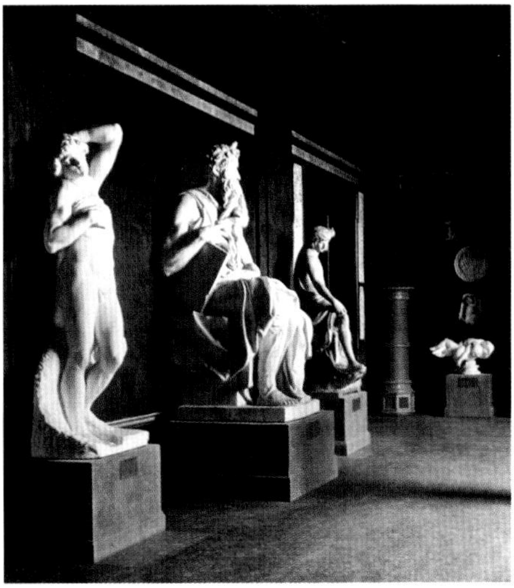

10| Josef Löwy, Plaster casts of Michelangelo's *Moses* and *Dying Prisoner* at the Akademie der bildenden Künste, Vienna. Photograph, c. 1870

55 Lloyd 1863; cf. letter of 20th October 1912 from Sigmund Freud to Sándor Ferenczi, in: Freud / Ferenczi 1993, p. 135. On this and the following points: Jones 1955, pp. 109–10.

(Fig. 10): "I'm now seeking to obtain permission to visit the museum of the Akademie der bildenden Künste, where there is a large plaster cast".[56]

It was presumably in this connection that Freud acquired a small copy of the *Moses*. For, on 3rd November, he wrote again to Ferenczi: "I'm still working on the Moses, of which there is now here, too, a plaster cast".[57] In the text of his *Moses* article, however, Freud was to criticise the cast at the Akademie because the Tablets of the Law, complete with spur, were recorded there in a manner that was "altogether incorrect".[58]

In the course of these studies Freud's Welsh supporter (and later biographer), the neurologist and psychoanalyst Ernest Jones, while in Florence in late October, sent him two photographs of sculptural works to be found in that city's Duomo: one of these was Donatello's *Saint John*, the other probably Nanni di Banco's *Saint Luke*.[59] Freud was evidently again concerned with the positioning of the Tablets of the Law. Jones was in fact about to leave Florence for Rome. Informed of these plans, Freud wrote to him on 15th November to congratulate him on his good fortune: "I envy you for se[e]ing Rome so soon and so early in life. Bring my deepest devotion to Moses and write me about him".[60] On 5th December Jones replied to tell Freud that he had most promptly fulfilled this request: "My first pilgrimage the day after my arrival was to convey your greetings to Moses, and I think he unbent a little from his haughtiness. What a statue!"[61] On 23rd December Jones playfully took up the notion of the animation of the marble figure in a letter to Freud accompanied by two new photographs of details from this work: "I enclose two photographs of Moses. Will you tell me if they are what you wanted. You will notice that the projecting pediment interferes inevitably with the view of the tables [= Tablets]. I examined the latter carefully, and one cannot say that there are fingerprints on them".[62] This response reveals that Freud was still preoccupied

56 Letter of 27th October 1912 from Sigmund Freud to Sándor Ferenczi, in: Freud / Ferenczi 1993, p. 140.

57 Letter of 3rd November 1912 from Sigmund Freud to Sándor Ferenczi, in: Freud / Ferenczi 1993, p. 147.

58 Sigmund Freund, "Der Moses des Michelangelo", in: *SFG*, vol. 14, p. 36.

59 Letter of 30th October 1912 from Ernst Jones to Sigmund Freud, in: Freud / Jones 1993, pp. 165–66, here 165. On this point: Grubrich-Simitis 2004, pp. 18–19. Cf. also letter of 8th November 1912 from Sigmund Freud to Ernest, in: Freud / Jones 1993, pp. 170–72, here 172: "Your two photographs have shaken much of the confidence in my interpretation [...].

60 Letter of 15th November 1912 from Sigmund Freud to Ernest Jones, in: Freud / Jones 1993, pp. 176–77, here 177.

61 Letter of 5th December 1912 from Ernest Jones to Sigmund Freud, in: Freud / Jones 1993, pp. 179–80, here 179.

62 Letter of 23rd December 1912 from Ernest Jones to Sigmund Freud, in: Freud / Jones 1993, pp. 183–84, here 184.

with the positioning of the Tablets of the Law, to which he had paid particular attention in several of the entries in his notebook, and in connection with which he had carefully examined the plaster cast at the Akademie in Vienna. The fact that there was a slight space between the right armpit and the upper end of the Tablets was of particular significance within Freud's interpretation because it offered a further hint at a danger that the Tablets, being held in place insufficiently securely, might inadvertently have been allowed to fall.[63]

In Freud's next letter, dated 26th December, in which he thanked Jones for the photographs, he again asked for a more precise account of particular aspects of the Tablets: "Thanks for your two photographs of Moses. They show as much as may reasonably be expected. If I may trouble you for something more – it is more than indiscrete – let me say I want a reproduction – even by drawing – of the remarkable lower contour of the tables [= Tablets], running thus in a note of mine" (Fig. 11).[64]

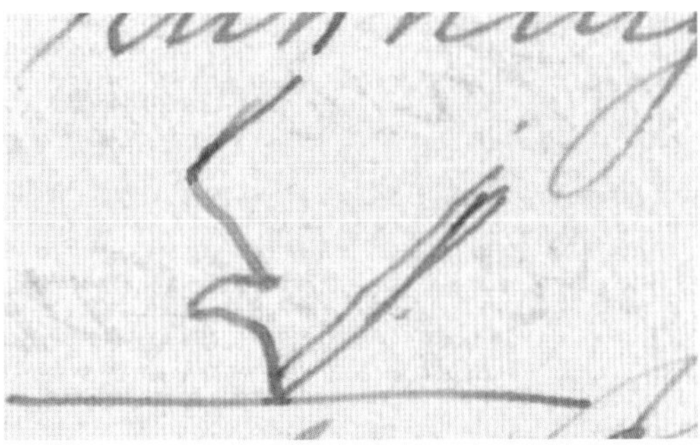

11| Sigmund Freud, Sketch of the Tablets of the Law with spur, letter of 26th December 1912 to Ernest Jones. Sigmund Freud Papers, Library of Congress, Washington, D. C.

The drawing in question was a copy of that sketch in the notebook in which Freud had recorded the spur visible at the lower edge of one of the Tablets (see Fig. 9). Evidently, Freud was now seeking reliable evidence for his assumption that this spur was indeed a decorative device added to the upper part of the Tablets (these being held by Moses in an inverted position) where it may initially have served as a support for the right hand. The reason for Freud's request to Jones lay in the fact that the presence of the spur would have made plausible the entirety of Freud's projection of the actions that had preceded the depicted moment: the right hand delving into the beard, the perceived danger that the Tablets might fall, and the consequent instinctive inward pressing of the upper right arm.

63 Freud's notebook no. 10, fols. 10.98–10.101, in: Freud 2021, p. 243.

64 Letter of 26th December 1912 from Sigmund Freud to Ernest Jones, in: Freud / Jones 1993, p. 186–87.

Identification with Michelangelo's *Moses*

In a letter to Jones of 1st January 1913, Freud reported that he would break off his correspondence with Carl Gustav Jung because, in the light of what had become of that friendship, it was simply "not worth the ink".[65] The mood of intransigeance already informing these words was to dominate much of Freud's life throughout that year, issuing in September, at the IV International Psychoanalytic Congress, in Munich, in the irreparable rupture that he would thereafter count as one of the most bitter disappointments of his life.

On the final day of the Congress, 9th September, Freud left Munich for Rome, where he intended to stay for three weeks. And there he was finally freed from his sense of bitterness. On 21st September he assured his pupil and confidant Karl Abraham: "In the incomparable beauty of Rome, my mood has improved and I've rediscovered a desire to work".[66] Two decades later, in 1933, in a letter to the psychoanalyst Edoardo Weiss (who was to have a leading role in the introduction of Freudian theory and practice to Italy),[67] Freud recalled that it was in around 1913 that he had again began to concern himself with sculpture, and that he had "gone daily to the church [San Pietro in Vincoli] to stand before the statue, had studied it, measured it, drawn it".[68]

Two postcards sent to Ferenczi from Rome in 1913 reveal that there was now more at play here than merely the analysis of a work of art. On 11th September, a day after his arrival, Freud concluded his message with the words: "Haven't yet

65 Letter of 1st January 1913 from Sigmund Freud to Ernest Jones, in: Freud / Jones 1993, pp. 189–90, here 190.

66 Letter of 21st September 1913 from Sigmund Freud to Karl Abraham, in: Freud / Abraham 1980, p. 146.

67 Zapperi 2016, pp. 31–36.

68 Letter of 12th April 1933 from Sigmund Freud to Edoardo Weiss, in: Freud 1968, p. 431. Freud's statement has been frequently discussed in the literature. It has been claimed that, in retrospect, he confused the years 1913 and 1912. Freud's memory of events occurring 20 years earlier is technically inaccurate in that it was not in 1913, but in 1907, that he had spent "three lonely weeks in September" in Rome. In 1913, by contrast, he spent only two weeks there and he was, moreover, not alone, but accompanied by his sister-in-law Minna Bernays. This has led to the assumption that Freud was here confusing the dates and that what he claimed of the year 1913 related in fact to 1912 (Freud 1968, p. 520, 1933, note 1; Freud 1969b, editorial note, p. 196; *Sigmund Freud* 1985, p. 205; D'Angelo 2020, p. 270). In any case, Freud's observation was also inexact because in 1912 there were only a few days during which he would have been able, on his own, to devote himself to Michelangelo's figure. It should thus be assumed that the reference should have been to the year 1913, but that Freud was also drawing on his memories of earlier occasions. (This is the view adopted by Christfried Tögel, who does not call into question Freud's references to the year 1913 [*Sigmund Freud* 2003, p. 372; and Tögel 2019, p. 147]).

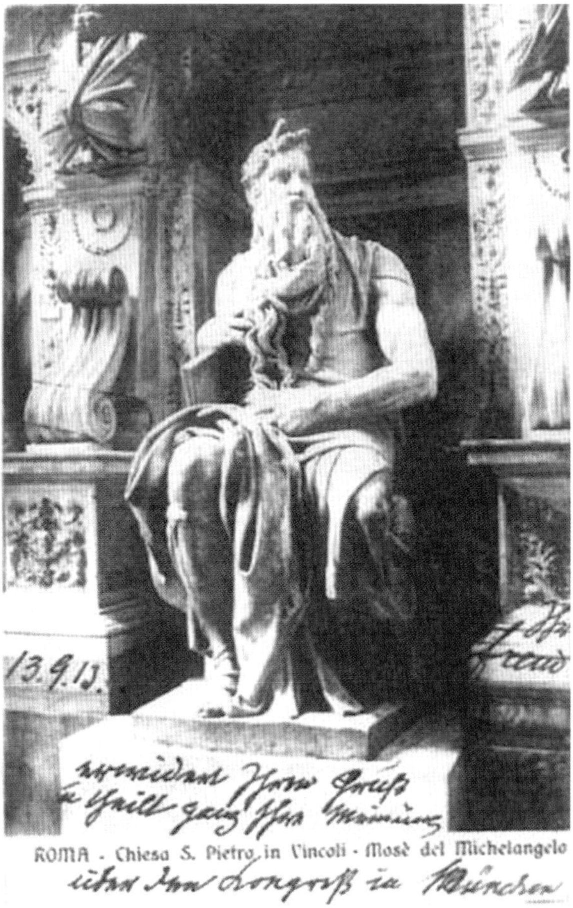

12| Postcard of Michelangelo's *Moses* sent on 13th September 1913 by Sigmund Freud to Sándor Ferenczi. Vienna, Österreichische Nationalbibliothek

visited Trevi and Moses".[69] The fact that Freud here spontaneously spoke, as in a single breath, of the *Moses* and the Trevi Fountain – the latter the sight of sights to see during any visit to Rome – reveals that, while in Munich, he must have talked with Ferenczi about Michelangelo's figure as the sight that was, for him, obligatory. Two days later, on 13th September, in a second postcard (Fig. 12),[70] Freud revealed the full extent of what Michelangelo's figure had become for him.

69 Postcard of 11th September 1913 from Sigmund Freud to Sándor Ferenczi, in: Freud / Ferenczi 1993, p. 243.

70 Postcard of 13th September 1913 from Sigmund Freud to Sándor Ferenczi, in: Freud / Ferenczi 1993, p. 244.

The image shows the *Moses* viewed diagonally from the right and is printed with the caption: "ROMA – Chiesa S. Pietro in Vincoli – Mosè del Michelangelo". On the bases of the powerful volutes that flank the figure, Freud has inscribed the date "13.9.13" and a valediction in the form "*Ihr Freud*" [Yours, Freud]. The real message, however, appears to come not from Freud, but from Michelangelo's figure itself. For it is the *Moses* that speaks the inscribed words: "[Moses] reciprocates your greeting and entirely shares your view of the Congress in Munich". In the tradition of ostensibly inanimate figures "speaking" in the first person singular and thereby attesting to their own latent vitality,[71] the *Moses* here speaks in place of Freud. Through this wordplay – simultaneously frivolous and earnest – Michelangelo's marble figure becomes Freud's alter ego.

This postcard to Ferenczi reveals that the marble figure has been transformed into an embodiment of Freud himself.[72] The salutation "*Ihr Freud*" shows that, at this moment, a merging of person and sculptural work had taken place. Just as the *Moses* here appears to utter Freud's own words, Freud implicitly presents himself as the sculpture's human reincarnation. Finally, the reference to the Munich Congress affirms that C. G. Jung was bound into the mix as a malevolent third party. Ferenczi evidently understood these allusions and metamorphoses. In his response to Freud, he thanked him warmly for the words addressed to him by the marble figure: "I thank you heartily for both postcards and was most honoured by the greeting from Moses".[73]

In the aforementioned letter that Freud sent to Karl Abraham on 21st September, that is to say over a week after the postcards sent to Ferenczi, Freud mentioned that "in what free time I have, between visits to museums – churches – the Campagna – I've manged to complete the text of a lecture on my book on totem and taboo, an extension of the paper I gave at the Congress, and a sketch for an essay on narcissism".[74] While Freud was at work on planning his article on Michelangelo's *Moses*, that is to say, he was also preoccupied with the other texts cited here. If Freud, at the point where he was intensely focused on the *Moses*, defined narcissism as the re-projection on to the ego of the libido stirred by the

71 Bredekamp 2015, pp. 65–95.

72 Grubrich-Simitis 2004, p. 16; Bergstein 2006, p. 172; Bredekamp 2006, pp. 35–36; Bergstein 2010, p. 110.

73 Letter of 15th September 1913 from Sándor Ferenczi to Sigmund Freud, in: Freud / Ferenczi 1993, p. 245.

74 Letter of 21st September 1913 from Sigmund Freud to Karl Abraham, in: Freud / Abraham 1980, p. 146.

object of affection[75] he acted on his own diagnosis. The outcome was that Jung's own work was treated altogether negatively in that essay.[76]

On 21st September, the very date on which Freud wrote to Karl Abraham of his work on narcissism, he told Jones how deeply engaged he was in his now personally inflected research on the *Moses*: "I have visited old Moses again and got confirmed in my explication of his position, but something in the comparative material you collected for me, did shake my confidence which is not yet restored".[77] It is clear that Freud had been troubled by the fact that the other figures brought to his attention by Jones were not holding the Tablets of the Law as Freud had described them being held by Michelangelo's *Moses*; they were, that is to say, not pressed into the right armpit, but held rather loosely with one end resting on the upper thigh. Nonetheless, evidently enthused by his own new eagerness for study and stimulated by the notion of his own merging with the sculpted figure, Freud made rapid progress with his article. He was later to report to Jones that he had completed it on 1st January 1914.[78]

Ernest Jones, in his biography of Freud, writes of this episode: "One cannot avoid the pretty obvious conclusion that at this time and probably before, Freud had identified himself with Moses and was striving to emulate the victory over passions that Michelangelo had depicted in his stupendous achievement".[79] One can refine on this assessment in so far as the connection with Michelangelo is first evident in the photograph taken by Martin Freud in 1906 (see Fig. 4), even though the specific connection with Michelangelo's *Moses* becomes fully evident in September 1913. By that date the founder of psychoanalysis clearly felt himself to be a living reincarnation of the marble figure.

75 Sigmund Freud, "Zur Einführung des Narzissmus", in: *SFG*, vol. 14, pp. 47–73, here 50.

76 Sigmund Freud, "Zur Einführung des Narzissmus", in *SFG*, vol. 14, pp. 51–52.

77 Letter of 21st September 1913 from Sigmund Freud to Ernest Jones, in: Freud / Jones 1993, pp. 226–27, here 227.

78 Letter of 3rd January 1914 from Sigmund Freud to Ernest Jones, in: Freud / Jones 1993, p. 252: "I have finished Moses the first day of this year and liked it better while writing than before".

79 Jones 1955, p. 411.

Freud's reluctant publication of the *Moses* article: 1914

In Freud's aforementioned letter of 1933 to Edoardo Weiss, he characterised his stance towards the article on the *Moses* as veering between joy and scruple:

> "The Italian [translation of] 'Moses' brought me great joy. My relationship with this work is somewhat like that one might have with a love-child. During three lonely weeks in September 1913, I went every day to stand in front of the statue, I studied it, measured it, drew it until I finally understood that which I then dared, in my text, to express only anonymously. It was only much later that I legitimised this non-analytical child".[80]

It is particularly telling that Freud should describe his article as a "love-child", in other words the fruit of an illicit relationship, of the sort one would be rather inclined to conceal than to reveal. If he then also described his text as "non-analytical", this was presumably because the quarrel with Jung had also played a part in his research into Michelangelo's marble figure. The intimate and personal nature of Freud's response to his subject would necessarily contradict the methodical insistence upon the neutrality of the analyst. And it may well have been this that induced Freud to insist that the article be published anonymously.

As is evident from Freud's letter to Ferenczi of 3rd January 1914, this ostensibly unreasonable request was met by misunderstanding among Freud's comrades-in-arms: "I have completed [the text on] the Moses and I still don't know why they protest so vigorously against my preference for anonymity".[81] Three days later Freud sent an explanatory note to Karl Abraham: "1. It is only a joke, 2. Shame at the evident amateurishness of the essay, 3. Lastly because my doubt about my conclusion is stronger than usual; it is only because of editorial pressure (Rank and Sachs) that I have consented to publication at all".[82] Even in writing to Ernest Jones, Freud sought to present the article as a joke: "P.S. Why should I disgrace the Moses by putting my name to it? It is a fun [= a joke] and perhaps no bad one".[83]

80 Letter of 12th April 1933 from Sigmund Freud to Edoardo Weiss, in: Freud 1968, p. 431.

81 Letter of 3rd January 1914 from Sigmund Freud to Sándor Ferenczi, in: Freud / Ferenczi 1993, p. 272.

82 Letter of 6th January 1914 from Sigmund Freud to Karl Abraham, here cited after Jones 1955, p. 410. In the volume of correspondence between Freud and Abraham (Freud / Abraham 1980) this letter is not included.

83 Letter of 16th January 1914 from Sigmund Freud to Ernest Jones, in: Freud / Jones 1993, pp. 255–56, here 256.

Freud's decision to describe his article as a "joke" might perhaps even be understood as an ironic justification of his own efforts to bring psychoanalysis to that very subject;[84] and, in that respect, this characterisation was a clever move. But Freud's real reason for encouraging potential readers to approach the text in a spirit of scepticism was concealed from those outside his immediate circle. Evidently, Freud wished to suppress the fact that, within a text ostensibly addressing a work of sculpture by Michelangelo, there lingered a second question that related to his own life: how to address the trauma of being betrayed, as he saw it, by Jung? – through "murdering" the son or through attaining mastery over the self.

Freud's misgivings grew stronger when, in discussion with artists (from whom he had hoped to receive support for his own interpretation of the *Moses*), he was forced to comprehend that they were primarily interested in questions of form, and not in implicit psychological drama. On 8th February 1914 he wrote to Ernest Jones of his annoyance at such one-sidedness:

> "In the Moses affair I am growing negative again, the last artist I consulted showed me what the way of artists in such matters is and made me afraid of too sharp an interpretation. Meaning is but little with these men, all they care [about] is line, shape, agreement of contours. They are given up to the Lustprinzip. I prefer to be cautious".[85]

By the end of February, as Freud reported to Ferenczi, things had reached a point where commitment to one course or another was required: "On Friday, 20th of this month, there is to be an official Moses Evening, where a decision will be taken regarding the fate of this gamble".[86] Present here, in addition to the members of the editorial board, was to be Max Pollak, who had prepared the drawings that would accompany Freud's text.[87] The meeting resulted in the decision that the article would be published, in April 1914, in the third volume of the journal *Imago*.

This important periodical, devoted to non-clinical applications of psychoanalysis, had been founded by Freud together with Otto Rank, Secretary of the Wiener Psychologische Gesellschaft, and himself a close confidant of Freud, and Hanns Sachs, a Viennese lawyer and psychoanalyst, who in 1913, in collaboration

84 Sigmund Freud, "Der Witz und seine Beziehung zum Unbewussten", in: *SFG*, vol. 9, pp. 173–391.

85 Letter of 8th February 1914 from Sigmund Freud to Ernest Jones, in: Freud / Jones 1993, pp. 260–61.

86 Letter of 15th February 1914 from Sigmund Freud to Sándor Ferenczi, in: Freud / Ferenczi 1993, p. 285.

87 Letter of 15th February 1914 from Sigmund Freud to Sándor Ferenczi, in: Freud / Ferenczi 1993, p. 285.

with Rank, had published a text of fundamental importance on the connection between psychoanalysis and the Humanities.[88] Even the journal's sub-title – signalling the great interest of psychoanalysis in this broader context – would have indicated that Freud's article must have seemed as if destined for its pages; but evidently Freud himself continued to wonder whether, in agreeing to publish, he would not in fact be doing a disservice both to the goals of psychoanalysis and to the reputation of the journal. Although one of those closest to him, Karl Abraham, writing at the start of April, told him that every astute and informed reader would "recognise the lion's claw",[89] making it all but pointless to publish anonymously, the text nonetheless appeared as the work of "…".

In the circumstances, the editorial remark that appeared at the foot of the first page seems almost parodic in its attempt to distance the journal from Freud's text: "The editors did not wish to stand in the way of the inclusion of a contribution that is, strictly speaking, not in compliance with the journal's programme, because its author, who is known to them, is himself close to analytical circles and because his manner of thinking has something in common with the methods of pychoanalysis".[90] This formulation, which characterises the editorial board as graciously and generously agreeing to publish a dilettante's essentially unworthy effort, doubtless provoked no end of amusement in Rank and Sachs. For Freud, however, who had in fact devised it himself, there was nothing ironic about it.[91] He still thought his own ideas about Michelangelo's *Moses* to be problematic. It was only in 1924, during the preparation of an edition of his complete works, that he agreed to add his name to the text.[92]

88 Rank & Sachs 1913. The title of the journal was taken from that of the novel by the Swiss writer Carl Spitteler, who had made the unconscious an actor in his narrative (Spitteler 1906; cf. Gay 1988, pp. 311–12).

89 Letter of 2nd April 1914 from Karl Abraham to Sigmund Freud, in: Freud / Abraham 1980, p. 165; cf. Grubrich-Simitis 2004, p. 23.

90 Sigmund Freud, "Der Moses des Michelangelo", in: *SFG*, vol. 14, p. 21.

91 Grubrich-Simitis 2004, pp. 37–38.

92 Freud 1924.

3. Analysis of film and the distinction of hands

The message of the beard

The observations made by Freud, in September 1912, on the right hand of Michelangelo's *Moses* led to a breakthrough in his realisation that the seemingly motionless marble in fact held within itself a sequence of agitated movements. Freud observed in detail every aspect of the motility of the figure. In this, however, there lay only the starting point for a study of the form of the beard itself (Fig. 13), which was to distinguish the essence of Freud's analysis.

It can hardly have been a coincidence that, three months after Freud's intensive studies of the forms of the right hand and the beard of the *Moses*, a remark made by C. J. Jung on 18th December 1912 should so swiftly be followed by Freud's decision to pay greater attention to the rendering of the beard itself. In a letter of that date, Jung accused Freud of feeling neurotically compelled to treat all his pupils like children, fit only to be educated and disciplined, and not permitted to

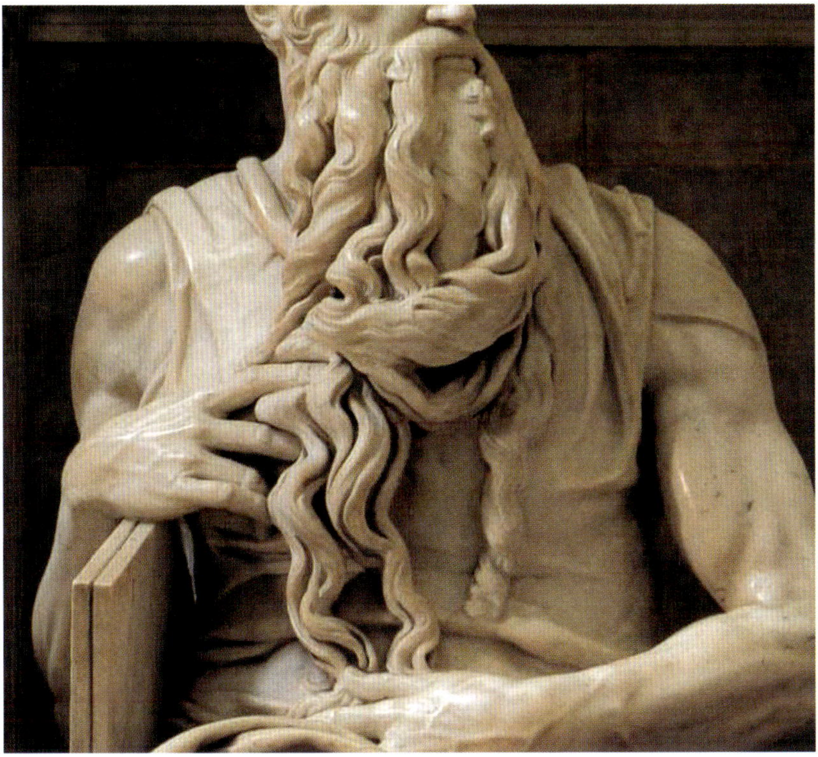

13| Michelangelo, *Moses*: right hand, beard. 1513–15. Marble. Rome, San Pietro in Vincoli

contradict what they had been told. Now viewing ironically Freud's claim, of January 1909, that he identified with the biblical Moses,[93] Jung turned this against him: "Being reduced to subservience, none of us has dared to pluck the prophet by his beard [...]".[94]

Within a few days Freud had contested Jung's allegations, albeit at first rather mildly. But, with little further provocation, on 3rd January he went much further towards what was soon to become a definitive break: "I propose that we abandon our personal relations entirely. I shall lose nothing by it [...] and you have everything to gain [...]".[95] It was, however, surely in response to Jung's allusion to the beard of the prophet that the notes Freud had initially devoted to the beard of Michelangelo's *Moses* were to be reworked and greatly extended for his article. For there he was to appraise that beard not as a sign of unquestionable authority, but as the means of communicating an inner conflict. The strands of beard hair did not equate to a corporeal manifestation of single-mindedness; rather, they registered the struggle of the corporeal entity with itself. Such were the insights that Freud then followed in his analysis of the beard. And, if this effort to understand the movement of the fingers and the strands of beard hair was such that his words were later to be acclaimed as one of the great passages of writing in German, then this must also in part have been due to the fact that, in this passage in particular, Freud was responding to Jung's accusations.

In order to acquire a sense of the rhythm of those sentences that track the cascading beard hair, one should examine that part in the text that traces how this movement also registers that of the entire upper body:

> "The thick hanks of hair extending inwards from this last strand and reaching from there to the mid-point [of the beard], have known the strangest fate. They cannot follow the movement of the head towards the [figure's] left; they are constrained to create a gently unrolling curve, resembling a segment of a garland, which meets, then traverses, the hanks of hair at the inner right. They will of course be held in check by the right forefinger, even though they originate to the left of the mid-point, and in fact constitute the chief part of the left half of the beard. The beard as a whole thus appears as if cast to the figure's right, even though the head has turned abruptly to his left. At that place where the right forefinger exerts its pressure, a swirl of hair has formed;

93 See above, pp. 11–12.

94 Letter of 18th December 1912 from C. G. Jung to Sigmund Freud, in: Freud / Jung 1974, p. 594.

95 Letters of 22nd December 1912 and 3rd January 1913 from Sigmund Freud to C. G. Jung, in: Freud / Jung 1974, pp. 596 and 598–99.

> here, strands of hair from the left overlap with those from the right, both held in check by the forceful finger. It is only beyond this point that the hanks of hair break free from the restraining digit, in order now to fall vertically until their ends are captured in the open palm of the left hand resting in the figure's lap".[96]

Freud attends to every detail of the strands of beard hair with the phenomenological precision of an art historian like Adolph Goldschmidt, who compared the art of describing with the action of a fly crawling across the undulating surface of a work of sculpture.[97] Through establishing this interconnection of content and form, Freud was able to perceive, within the "frozen" marble figure, a principle of movement, in relation to which he could then develop his psychoanalytic interpretation.[98]

Within the apparently static seated pose of the *Moses* Freud perceived that several stages of movement were simultaneously present; and these he commissioned Max Pollak to visualise (Fig. 14). This painter and print-maker was a protégé of the publisher Hugo Heller, who had brought out the book version of Freud's *Totem and Taboo* and who published the journal *Imago*.[99] Pollak had also made the portrait etching (see Fig. 33) that Freud mentioned to Ferenczi, in a letter of 11th February 1914, in connection with the commissioned drawings: "Max Pollak, who 'etched' my portrait, has now also promised to provide the drawings".[100] Four days later, on 15th February, Freud was able to report that "Pollak, the artist, [has provided] very good drawings".[101] Freud's satisfaction with this outcome reveals that he was aware that his own verbal exposition, notwithstanding its almost insuperably precise and sensitive use of language, would not alone suffice to convey, in every particular, that which he wished his readers to understand. Pollak's drawings should, then, be understood as themselves integral to Freud's text.

The series opens (Fig. 14, D) with an outline drawing of that aspect of the figure of Michelangelo's *Moses* that Freud analyses in evolving his overall interpretation. The following three sketches, which show the entire upper body, distinguish sequential stages in the movement that, in Freud's view, ended with the figure in the pose in which it was encountered. According to Freud, the figure of

96 Sigmund Freud, "Der Moses des Michelangelo", in: *SFG*, vol. 14, p. 33.

97 Sears 2007, p. 290.

98 Reiche 2001, pp. 9–10; cf. Grubrich-Simitis 2004, pp. 38–39.

99 Molnar 2006, p. 24.

100 Letter of 11th February 1914 from Sigmund Freud to Sándor Ferenczi, in: Freud / Ferenczi 1993, p. 283.

101 Letter of 15th February 1914 from Sigmund Freud to Sándor Ferenczi, in: Freud / Ferenczi 1993, p. 285.

Moses initially embodies an air of unruffled majesty; this is, however, disturbed by the noise of the Israelites dancing around the Golden Calf (Fig. 14, 1). In response, the figure's left hand shoots out while the right, seeking a means to divert a surge of aggression, clutches involuntarily at the massive beard (Fig. 14, 2):

> "If, in the figure of *Moses*, the strands of beard hair to the left are partially held in place by the forefinger of the right hand, then this may perhaps be understood as what remains of a relationship between the right hand and the left half of the beard that, a few moments earlier, had been much closer. The right hand had then perhaps grasped the beard far more energetically, had reached as far as its left edge; and, as it withdrew to the position where one now finds it, a part of the beard followed it and now bears witness to the movement that had just occurred [(Fig. 14, 3)]. The garlands of the beard may be viewed as traces of the path followed by the hand".[102]

In addition, the left hand presses on the body's centre of energy, the stomach. In this interpretation, Michelangelo's *Moses* appears so undisturbed not because it has yet to break into a paroxysm of wrath, but because it is, even now, repressing an eruption of emotion. In Freud's view, Michelangelo depicts this figure not *before* the event (an outburst of anger) but *after* its successful prevention.

Freud was to return to this central element in his interpretation. In 1927, three years after his article on Michelangelo's *Moses* had at last appeared under his name, he published a supplement to it in the form of an account of a bronze figure of Moses by the late 12th-century Flemish enamellist, goldsmith and sculptor Nicholas of Verdun. This had caught Freud's attention because it, too, employed the motif of the hand gripping the beard, thereby seeming to confirm the validity of his focus on the play of movement within the beard itself.[103] The earlier figure shows a moment of maximum emotional arousal, by contrast with the solution adopted by Michelangelo. Freud, resorting here to understatement, observes this distinction: "If my interpretation of the motif of the hand clasping the beard may be allowed, then the Moses from 1180 may be seen to depict a moment marked by the tempest of the passions, while the statue in San Pietro in

102 Sigmund Freud, "Der Moses des Michelangelo", in: *SFG*, vol. 14, p. 34.

103 Sigmund Freud, "Appendice sur: Le Moïse de Michel-Ange", in: *SFG*, vol. 18, pp. 445–48; Sigmund Freud, "Nachtrag zur Arbeit über den Moses des Michelangelo", in: *SFG*, vol. 18, pp. 449–50. It was in response to this last text, among others, that Macmillan and Swales developed their fundamental critique of Freud's text on Michelangelo's *Moses* (Macmillan & Swales 2003, pp. 62–66). This was, however, formulated without their being aware of the work of Franz-Joachim Verspohl, who had already posed and answered the questions they later raised (Verspohl 1991; and Verspohl 2001).

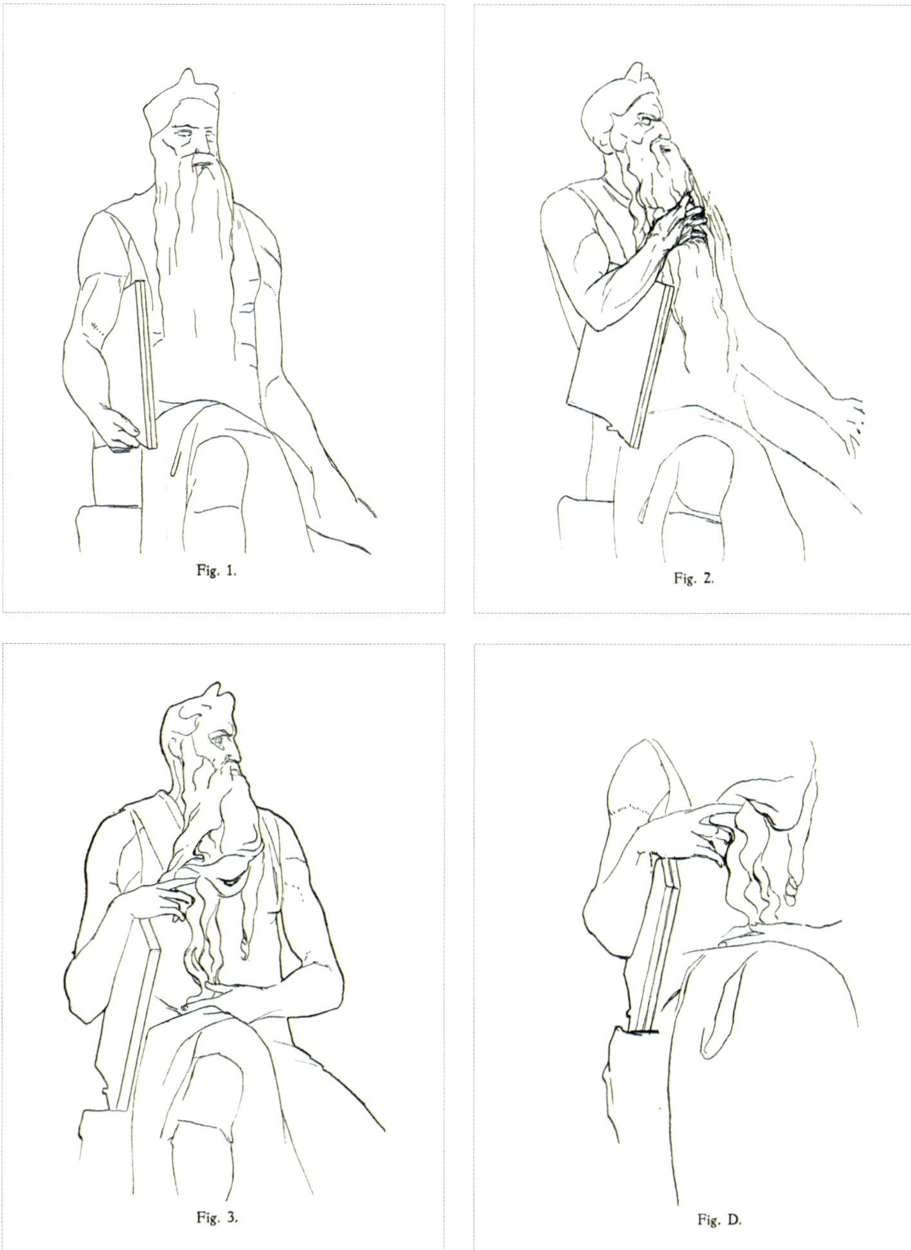

14| Max Pollak, drawings accompanying Freud's 1914 article on Michelangelo's *Moses*, showing projected sequence of prior movements

Vincoli shows the calm after the storm".[104] How significant for Freud was this opportunity to return to the subject of Michelangelo's figure is revealed by the fact that, after the first publication of the supplement, in French, he ensured that it also appear in German. The discovery of the small bronze figure must have seemed to Freud like a revelation. To his mind, it demonstrated that Michelangelo's *Moses* did not equate to a record of the psychological and emotional character of a single moment but was to be understood as the sum total of a completed sequence of both inner and outer movements.

The discovery of simultaneity

For Freud, the simultaneous record of a sequence of movements to be found within Michelangelo's *Moses* was akin to a cinematic record of the process of psychoanalysis. And the fact that he had been able, in his article on this figure, to capture his theory of the human psyche and its culturally creative capacities is itself in part to be explained by his own attraction to the cinema and his real feeling for visual seriality. In 1913, the writer and would-be psychoanalyst Lou Andreas-Salomé maintained, in a discussion with Freud, that "only the technique of film enables a swiftness in the sequence of images that almost corresponds to our own imaginative capacity and that, to a degree, imitates its volatility".[105]

Freud, nonetheless, doubted that film would ever adequately render states of mind. According to Ernest Jones, film in its material reality struck Freud as simply too concrete to be able to elucidate his theories of the psyche.[106] It is notable that Freud declined both the proposal he received from the Hollywood producer Samuel Goldwyn that they collaborate on a film about a number of history's celebrated love affairs, and the suggestion that he take part in the production of the educational film about psychoanalysis that Georg Wilhelm Pabst was to bring out in 1926, as *Geheimnisse einer Seele* [Secrets of a Soul][107] Freud felt that the medium of film, locked as it was into celluloid, was inappropriate as a substitute for the archiving capacity of the human mind.[108] For him, the true film of the psyche was

104 Sigmund Freud, "Nachtrag sur Arbeit über den Moses des Michelangelo", in: *SFG*, vol. 18, p. 450.

105 Andreas-Salomé 1983, p. 102.

106 "His main objection was his disbelief in the possibility of his abstract theories being presented in the plastic manner of a film" (Jones 1957, p. 121); cf. Doane 2002, p. 61 and note 46, pp. 241–42.

107 Friedberg 1990, pp. 41–42.

108 An alternative was offered to him in the children's drawing board known as the "*Wunderblock*", of which Freud wrote in an article of 1925; cf. Freud 1948. Using such a toy, lines incised with a stylus on greaseproof paper placed firmly upon a layer of wax would at first be visible but could then be made to "disappear" through peeling the paper off the wax

Michelangelo's *Moses*. Within the immobility of the marble, he had perceived the culmination of several stages of movement that, in their totality, truly captured the dynamism of psychic energies.

It may not entirely be a coincidence that Marcel Duchamp's painting of 1911 *Nude Descending a Staircase No. 1* (a still image of movement recorded as a sequence of poses) should emerge at almost exactly the time in which Freud was at work on his article on the *Moses*. Both achievements derive from essentially the same way of looking. And the fact that schemata appear to the human eye and brain as the visual stenogram of a continuous sequence had already been demonstrated by photographers such as Étienne Jules Marey and Eadweard Muybridge in the context of their own analyses of diverse forms of movement in time.[109] William S. Heckscher compared such procedures with the *montage* concept informing Aby Warburg's *Mnemosyne Image Atlas*.[110] Such a comparison is no less fitting in the case of Freud's visual theory of psychoanalysis.

And so, for Freud, Michelangelo's *Moses* remained the true film. His insistence on this point was by no means intended as an affirmation of his opposition to the avant-garde of the period. Rather, Freud wished to see the integration of that avant-garde into the realm of psychoanalysis. It was in the achievement of true sequentiality that he saw sculpture as superior to film. His concern was not with the linearity of a sequence of images, but with the contingency of that capacity of a work of art such as the *Moses* to "fill the gaps" occurring between the elements within such a sequence. It would be in each observer's own mental cinema that the movement so fully absorbed and so vividly present within such a work of sculpture would most compellingly recur.

Art history as psychoanalysis

Freud's determination to see a sculptural work in marble as an instance of true film was, ultimately, a reflection of the fact that he recognised that one of the precursors of psychoanalysis was the discipline of art history.[111] Freud was, in fact, much indebted to that discipline, and to a degree that, even now, seems astonishing. Although Freud had probably not come across Aby Warburg's dictum

layer, even though in fact being preserved, in a chaotic and palimpsestic fashion, within the latter. Cf. Friedberg 1990, p. 44; and Bredekamp 2006, p. 31.

109 Fuller 1980, p. 46.

110 Heckscher 1984, pp. 128–34. On the points of contact between Freud and Warburg, cf. Rose 2001; Bredekamp 2022.

111 Fundamental on this point: Ginzburg 1980. Also on the "search for traces": Metken 1977. Cf. Simmons 2006, pp. 220–27; Schmidgen 2018, pp. 68–82, 95–101.

"Der liebe Gott steckt im Detail"[112] [God dwells in the details], his recognition of the close observation of details as a sure means of training an art-historical eye testifies to a share in the same aims and the same methodology: in essence, a desire to detect in the microcosm of each detail a reflection of the macrocosm of the entire work of art:

> "Long before I had been able to learn anything of psychoanalysis, I had become aware that a Russian connoisseur, Ivan Lermolieff, whose first essays had appeared in German between 1874 and 1876, had caused quite a stir in the art galleries of Europe through calling into question the many pictures previously thought to be the work of a single painter, through explaining how to distinguish with certainty an original from a copy, and through establishing the existence of new, as yet unnamed, artists as those truly responsible for works now freed of their old attributions. He brought all this about through disregarding the general impression made by a painting and urging that curatorial attention be focused, instead, on characteristic, yet invariably overlooked, details such as the rendering of the fingernails, the earlobes, the halos [above the heads of saints] and other such unremarked things, to which a copyist was unlikely to pay attention, but which every artist depicted in a way that was peculiar to him".[113]

Following this explanation regarding the techniques of de-attribution and re-attribution employed by the "Russian connoisseur" – commonly known as the distinction of hands (that is to say, the distinction between diverse artists' tendencies in the treatment of details) – Freud reveals that the name Lermolieff is in fact a pseudonym used by an Italian, Giovanni Morelli. He then goes on to emphasise how close Morelli's art-historical technique is to the methods used in his own psychoanalytic practice: "I believe that his procedure is closely related to the technique of medical psychoanalysis. The latter, too, frequently attends to underrated or barely noticed aspects of a case, to be discovered within that which might so easily have been discarded, but within which is often to be detected that which is secret and that which is concealed".[114]

In writing here of Morelli, Freud refers to the volume published in 1897, *Della pittura italiana*.[115] But one may assume that he also studied other volumes

112 Mastroianni 2000.
113 Sigmund Freud, "Der Moses des Michelangelo", in: *SFG*, vol. 14, p. 32.
114 Sigmund Freud, "Der Moses des Michelangelo", in: *SFG*, vol. 14, p. 32.
115 Morelli 1897.

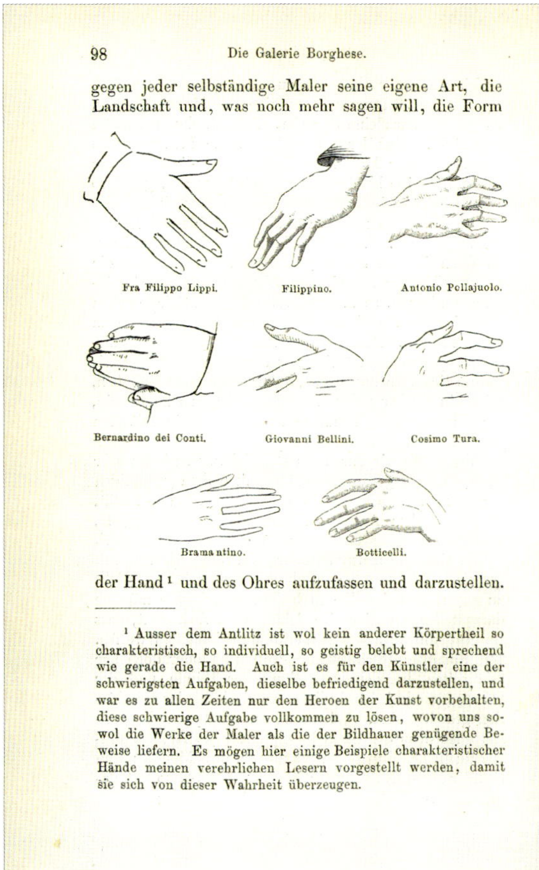

98 Die Galerie Borghese.

gegen jeder selbständige Maler seine eigene Art, die Landschaft und, was noch mehr sagen will, die Form

Fra Filippo Lippi. Filippino. Antonio Pollajuolo.

Bernardino dei Conti. Giovanni Bellini. Cosimo Tura.

Bramantino. Botticelli.

der Hand[1] und des Ohres aufzufassen und darzustellen.

[1] Ausser dem Antlitz ist wol kein anderer Körpertheil so charakteristisch, so individuell, so geistig belebt und sprechend wie gerade die Hand. Auch ist es für den Künstler eine der schwierigsten Aufgaben, dieselbe befriedigend darzustellen, und war es zu allen Zeiten nur den Heroen der Kunst vorbehalten, diese schwierige Aufgabe vollkommen zu lösen, wovon uns sowol die Werke der Maler als die der Bildhauer genügende Beweise liefern. Es mögen hier einige Beispiele charakteristischer Hände meinen verehrlichen Lesern vorgestellt werden, damit sie sich von dieser Wahrheit überzeugen.

15| Variation among artists in the depiction of hands. Anonymous book illustration to volume of 1890 by Ivan Lermolieff / Giovanni Morelli

illustrated in this fashion (Fig. 15).[116] In distinguishing the work of copyists and pupils from those of a master, Morelli always supplied the points he made with line drawings of the aspects to which he sought to draw attention, be they earlobes or fingers and fingernails.

Freud's encounter with such drawings would doubtless have prompted him to focus, in his study of Michelangelo's *Moses*, on the treatment of the figure's right hand and to record aspects of this in sketches of his own (see Fig. 7). Just as Freud, in his psychoanalytic practice, came to recognise that the essence of any situation was to be grasped through its unconscious, irrational expression – be this a motif glimpsed in a dream, or an irrepressible physical gesture – what mattered to him when he came to address Michelangelo's figure was what was to be gleaned through a study of the motility of the right forefinger and the strands

116 Lermolieff 1890, p. 98.

of beard hair. In focusing on such details, Freud effectively restored to art history the impulse that he had found within it. It was, then, the somewhat out-of-the-way clue to be found in Morelli's work that led Freud towards a sure test for "truth", which he then absorbed into his own psychoanalytic methods.

4. Biblical exegesis as a founding act of psychoanalysis

Michelangelo's wilfulness

The decisive aspect of Freud's analyses of the role of the right hand and of the beard of the *Moses* lay in his realisation that Michelangelo, in devising this figure, had not sought to visualise the episode as recounted in the Bible. The implicit narrative context is here, rather, an invention that effectively adds an entirely new scene to the biblical account. Freud's regard for the *Moses* was, indeed, all the greater in that this figure attested to Michelangelo's daring in contradicting not only the account in *Exodus*, but also the art-historical tradition deriving from that.

Cosimo Rosselli's contribution to the sequence of Moses frescoes in the Sistine Chapel, which Michelangelo will have viewed countless times while at work on the Sistine Chapel Ceiling, had itself faithfully depicted the scene in which Moses smashes the Tablets of the Law in his fury upon discovering that the Israelites had taken to worshipping an idol. According to Freud, Michelangelo's figure refrained from smashing the Tablets because the artist had

> "added to the tomb of the Pope another Moses, who is superior to that of history and tradition. He reworked the motif of the broken Tablets of the Law: here they are not broken by Moses in his wrath. There persists the threat that they might be broken, but also the sense of wrath appeased or to be in some way deflected. By this means, he has added something new, something super-human to the figure of Moses, and the massive body and powerful musculature are only the corporeal means of expression for the greatest psychic achievement of which a man is capable: the overcoming of his own passion in favour of, and in respect of, that to which he has solemnly dedicated himself".[117]

In view of the sacrilege committed by the Israelites, it is understandable that the Moses of the biblical account should react more or less instinctively and give vent to his rage. In Freud's view, Michelangelo's *Moses* is capable of self-control, and is

117 Sigmund Freud, "Der Moses des Michelangelo", in: *SFG*, vol. 14, p. 42.

thus not prone to precarious sudden movements. This was the essence of Freud's interpretation, and it was the argument to which he was to return in the first section of his last book, *Moses and Monotheism*:

> "In an act of inspired insight, Michelangelo shows us the man who is enraged at the people's worship of idols, but who elects not to give way to his fury out of respect for the Tablets of the Law then in his keeping, indeed his grasp. Had he given way to his passion, leapt up and stormed off, these would have smashed. But Michelangelo did not flinch here from breaking with tradition [...]".[118]

In this interpretation, Michelangelo's *Moses* retains a hold on his emotion even as it threatens to spill over, reasserting a spirit of self-control and the application of reason. Given the conflict with C. G. Jung, and as mentioned earlier, such a conclusion also held a message for Freud himself: he should focus single-mindedly upon his work and resist every temptation to give vent to his anger.

The wrong moment

While Freud's chief focus on the inner motility of Michelangelo's *Moses* was in every respect justified, he did, nonetheless, commit a flagrant error (albeit one he shared with most other commentators) in attempting to specify the moment within the biblical narrative that would have served as Michelangelo's starting point. He assumed that Michelangelo intended to depict Moses at that moment when he beheld the apostasy of his people. The clue that this was not Michelangelo's intention is to be found in the horns that spring from the head of his *Moses*. These signify the beams of light that, according to the biblical account (*Exodus*: 34, 29), were a mark of his direct contact with God, on Mount Sinai.[119] These, however, attested not to the meeting during the first ascent (on returning from which Moses was to discover the Israelites dancing around the Golden Calf), but to that during the second (when Moses, having smashed the first set of Tablets, received another).

This shift in the chronology does not, however, impact upon the psychodynamic corporeal movement that Freud analyses in his account in so forceful and, at the same time, so empathetic a fashion.[120] In spite of Freud's error, his interpretation remains persuasive because the decisive motif within his own

118 Here cited after Grubrich-Simitis 2004, p. 103.
119 Blum 2020, pp. 49–51.
120 This revision is owed to Franz-Joachim Verspohl (Verspohl 1991).

formal analysis remains the beard. Franz-Joachim Verspohl was able, through reference to the apparent slippage of the figure's left foot, to add something more to this correct identification of the episode to which Michelangelo intended to refer. It was at the moment when Moses received from God the second set of Tablets that God had declared that his servant would not himself live to see the Promised Land.[121] The equanimity of Moses was even more likely to be disturbed by this knowledge than by anger at the apostasy of the Israelites. But it is precisely on account of the simultaneous occurrence of the reception of the Tablets and the new insight into the time of his own death that the energy of the inner agitation thereby provoked palpably persists, even though largely suppressed through the figure's mastery over its own immense physical power. And so Michelangelo does far more than merely depart from the biblical narrative. In an intuitive foreshadowing of the Freudian notion of sublimation, he here chisels in marble the foundations of psychoanalysis 400 years before their theoretical elaboration.

121 Cf. the account, which agrees on this point, in Grubrich-Simitis 2004, pp. 69–95.

II FREUD'S COLLECTION AS AN INSTRUMENT FOR ANALYSIS

1. Freud as a collector before his 1914 article

The example of Jean-Martin Charcot

The extreme attention to detail in Freud's observations on the figure of *Moses* – and here, above all, regarding the form of the beard, the right hand and the spur on one of the Tablets of the Law – gives the impression that his own fingers had in fact touched its marble surface. And, in view of the long periods of time that he spent observing and drawing this figure, it is not altogether beyond the bounds of possibility that they had indeed been able to do so. Close proximity is also suggested by his sketch of the fingers, in particular the forefinger, of the right hand (see Fig. 7).

The small sculpted figures from Antiquity that Freud began collecting a good 15 years before he embarked upon his studies of Michelangelo, were of course at all times accessible to his touch. As Hanns Sachs observed, Freud barely uttered a statement of any significance without having one of his statuettes in his hand: "Freud had the habit of taking one or another piece of his collection from its place, and of examining it by sight and touch while he was talking".[1]

An early influence on Freud's approach to collecting would have been his experience during the winter of 1885 / 86, which he spent in Paris, on the staff of the celebrated neurologist Jean-Martin Charcot at the hospital where the latter both worked and taught, the Pitié-Salpêtrière. In advance of this period Freud had been unaware that the focus of Charcot's interests had shifted from research into the organic causes of mental disturbance to the study of neurotic states themselves. Freud was immensely impressed by Charcot's lectures on this subject.[2] But he was also no less moved than inspired by Charcot's readiness to communicate his liberal views and by the trust that he placed in his young colleague from

1 Sachs 1945, p. 99.
2 Tögel 1994, pp. 52–55.

Vienna in agreeing to Freud's proposal that he translate into German the third volume of the *Leçons sur les maladies du système nerveux*. In November 1885 Freud felt able to confide in his fiancée, Martha Bernays, that "no other person has ever had such an effect upon me".[3]

This was becoming especially true as regards Charcot's collections. In collaboration with Parisian colleagues, Charcot had assembled at the Salpêtrière a large group of items directly related to medical practice. In terms of the range of the objects here brought together, this was not unlike a traditional cabinet of curiosities. But it had a further dimension in that Charcot and his colleagues intended their patients, in as far as this was feasible and likely to be of service to enlightening comparison, to participate as living exhibits. Through this Musée Charcot, the strong Parisian tradition of museums conveying knowledge on every aspect of the natural world was enriched through the addition of a laboratory of images that stood at the service of psychology. The collection was no less remarkable for effectively removing the distinction between exhibits and patients.[4]

Freud was even more impressed by the collection installed in Charcot's own palatial home, to which he was invited initially to collect from Charcot the material he was to translate, and then later to dine. In the two spacious rooms that comprised Charcot's "study", Freud was altogether overwhelmed by the sheer height of the shelves of the "gigantic library", and, in particular, as he reported to Martha, by the collection itself:

> "In the rear section there is a stove, a table, cases of Indian and Chinese antiquities, and the walls (which seem to be painted a deep red) are covered in tapestries and pictures. As for other rooms of which I caught a glimpse on Sunday: there, too, the same extravagance of pictures, tapestries, carpets and curiosities – in short, it's a museum".[5]

This collection had been assembled through the combined efforts of Charcot and his wife, Victoire Augustine, and comprised works of art they had acquired with a great many decorative pieces supplied by the workshops owned by her.[6] Freud was so impressed by what he saw that he made a drawing of the "study" he had described to Martha, with particular attention to what he regarded as its exemp-

3 Letter of 24th November 1885, from Sigmund Freud to Martha Bernays, in: Freud 1968, p. 189.

4 Mayer 1998, p. 52; Mayer 2001, pp. 170–71. On this entire complex: Didi-Huberman 1997.

5 Letter of 20th January 1886 from Sigmund Freud to Martha Bernays, in Freud 1968, p. 200.

6 Mayer 1998, pp. 54–55.

lary aspects: the division into two sections, the bookshelves, a table upon which objects were displayed.[7]

Freud's first acquisitions

It was, without doubt, Freud's encounter with this private collection that led in due course to his becoming a collector himself. The items he acquired came chiefly from Antiquity: Egyptian, Greek and Roman. Over time, however, these were joined by objects from the Middle East and the Far East, and even America. In addition to sculpted figures (that is to say, nominally examples of fine art), there were also everyday objects, this being especially so in the case of material from the Aegean, for which Freud developed a particular liking.[8] By the time Freud left Vienna for London, in the early summer of 1938, he had, remarkably, assembled a total of between 2,000 and 3,000 items.

It would appear that it was in the mid-1890s, around a decade after his stay in Paris, that Freud embarked upon his own career as a collector, his financial situation then being such as to support his first moves in that direction. In August–September 1896 he made his second journey to Italy, where he spent time in Venice and in Tuscany. As already mentioned, he subsequently reported to his friend and colleague Wilhelm Fliess, that he had, while in Florence, acquired plaster casts of sculptural works, so as to keep alive the memory of that experience. Among these, in all probability, had been the *Dying Prisoner* (see. Fig. 4): "[Italy] was, for me, a source of extraordinary refreshment; I'm planning to become very rich so as to be able to repeat this journey. A Congress in Italy! (Naples, Pompeii)".[9]

In September 1897, at the most just a year after the acquisition of the plaster casts, Freud began to buy original pieces: to begin with, small sculpted figures from Antiquity. During his travels at that time in northern and central Italy he sent to Martha a postcard worded in the style of a telegram: "Cathedral. Etruscan graves, acquired antiquities, wonderful view".[10] These words in fact testify to Freud's first encounter with Riccardo Mancini, a dealer in antiquities who had had excavations carried out at an Etruscan necropolis (the Crocifisso del Tufo) located on and beneath his own land, near Orvieto (Fig. 16).[11]

7 Letter of 20th January 1886 from Sigmund Freud to Martha Bernays, in: Freud 1968, pp. 200–03; cf. Mayer 2001, p. 197.

8 D'Agata 1994; Marinelli 1998, pp. 11–12.

9 Letter of 6th December 1896 from Sigmund Freud to Wilhelm Fliess, in: Freud / Fliess 1986, p. 226.

10 Postcard of 9th September 1897 from Sigmund Freud to Martha Freud, in: *Sigmund Freud* 2003, p. 85.

11 Dennis 1878, vol. II, p. 43.

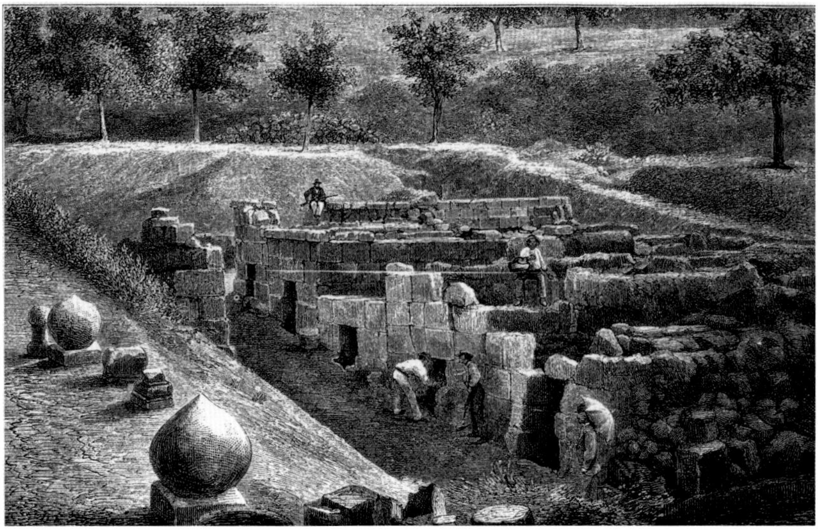

16| Anonymous, Crocifisso del Tufo: Etruscan necropolis near Orvieto. Heliogravure

Mancini had lost no time in establishing a business to sell the vessels and figures discovered by this means. For all the commercial success and the renown he thereby acquired, he nonetheless drew criticism from a number of archaeologists: for exhibiting the ruthlessness of a Heinrich Schliemann and, above all, for squandering Italy's Etruscan heritage.[12]

Freud, however, was nonetheless happy to profit from this dubious trade in antiquities. It is likely that it was from Mancini's collection that he acquired the Etruscan vessel that features in the so-called "thirst dream" recorded in *The Interpretation of Dreams* published in 1900: "I thus appropriately dreamt that my wife gave me to drink from a vessel; this vessel was a small Etruscan cinerary urn that I had brought home from a journey to Italy and had since given to someone as a present".[13]

Almost a year later, in August 1898, Freud reported to Wilhelm Fliess that, while in Innsbruck, he had bought "a small Roman statuette".[14] From this point on, as is revealed by a great many subsequent letters to Fliess, Freud intensified his collecting activity. In mid-July 1899 he reported that he was already in possession of numerous small sculptural works from Antiquity: "There are old gods, of

12 O'Donoghue 2019, pp. 91–95.

13 Sigmund Freud, "Die Traumdeutung", in: *SFG*, vol. 7, here p. 124. Cf. O'Donoghue 2019, p. 103–06; D'Angelo 2020, pp. 108–09.

14 Letter of 20th August 1898 from Sigmund Freud to Wilhelm Fliess, in: Freud / Fliess 1986, p. 352.

which I only recently acquired a few, among them a Janus, in stone, both of whose faces regard me with an air of superiority".[15] Writing again to Fliess two weeks later, Freud alluded both to a scholarly tradition dating back to the Renaissance and to the text on which he was himself then at work, in pointing out that such small sculpted figures might also serve a practical purpose. With explicit reference to the manuscript pages of what would soon become *The Interpretation of Dreams*, he observed: "My old and filthy gods, whom you fail to value, in fact participate – as paperweights – in my work".[16]

The seemingly magical relationship between sculpted figures and text at which Freud here hints – of particular relevance in the case of the work in question (so rich in references to Antiquity and to travel) – was in time to become a model for their role as images with true agency.[17] Less than a week later Freud wrote to Fliess from Berchtesgaden, which made him for the moment happy but which he would readily forsake, on the very next occasion of bad weather, for Salzburg, because, "the last time I was there, I stumbled upon a couple of Egyptian antiquities. These things excite me and speak to me of distant times and lands".[18] This observation, too, is suggestive of the auratic character that such objects were already beginning to have for Freud. They inspired him through rendering tactile, and thus immediately accessible, that which was historically or spatially remote.

Over the years Freud made a number of return visits to Riccardo Mancini. As of August 1902, it appears that the trade in antiquities was still flourishing.[19] In September 1907, however, Freud discovered that his Italian friend planned a change of direction. An entry in Freud's notebook reads: "The Antichità Mancini largely disappointing. I see I'll soon have to stop collecting. It's so hard to establish new connections".[20] Writing to his family on 17th September, he explained that he had "bought little, because there was little to be had [...] My friend Mancini wants to sell his olive orchard and his vineyard, beneath which there are still [the contents of] countless Etruscan graves to be retrieved. That would be a diverting and healthy occupation, but we of course have other work to do".[21]

15 Letter of 17th July 1899 from Sigmund Freud to Wilhelm Fliess, in: Freud / Fliess 1986, p. 397.

16 Letter of 1st August 1899 from Sigmund Freud to Wilhelm Fliess, in: Freud / Fliess 1986, p. 399. On this earlier use of items from a collection: Molnar 1998, pp. 41–42.

17 Cf. the overview in: D'Angelo 2020, pp. 315–18.

18 Letter of 6th August 1899 from Sigmund Freud to Wilhelm Fliess, in: Freud / Fliess 1986, p. 401. Cf. Kogel 2019, p. 74.

19 Letter of 30th August 1902 from Sigmund Freud to Martha Freud, in *Sigmund Freud* 2003, p. 155.

20 Freud's notebook no. 7, fol. 7.10, in: Freud 2021, p. 122.

21 Letter of 17th September 1907 from Sigmund Freud to his family, in: Sigmund Freud 2003, p. 216.

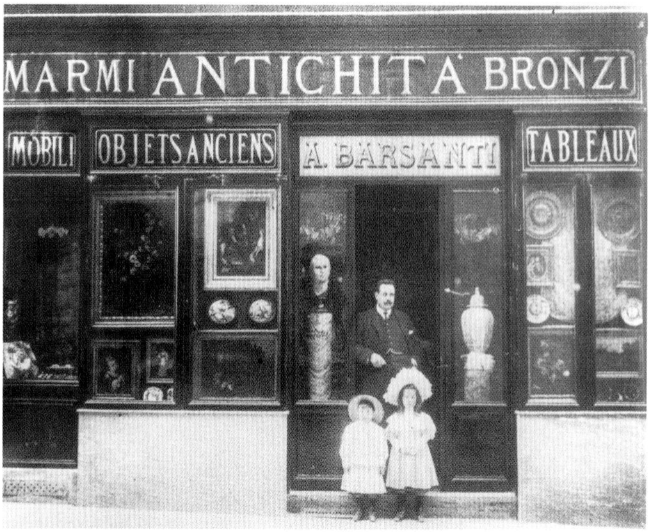

17| Claudia Barsanti, Store of Alfredo Barsanti, dealer in antiquities, at 48 Via Sistina, Rome

By the next day, however, Freud had already begun to overcome his disappointment: in a notebook entry for 18th September – the start of a stay in Rome – he registers his desire to visit a store located in the Palazzo Odescalchi: that of Attilio Simonetti, a dealer in antiquities.[22] As it proved, no purchases at all were possible when this plan was realised, five days later. Freud in due course felt able to laugh at the situation: "Man at Simonetti's store showed me all the treasures they had and assured me he could never think of selling them, but took pleasure in being able to show them". Then, as if commenting as an observer of this scene, Freud adds: "As for me: I was just wasting my time".[23]

While in Rome Freud sought out other dealers in antiquities from whom it might be possible to buy: among these were the collection of Alfredo Barsanti (at 48 Via Sistina, Fig. 17),[24] the Rainaldi art collection (at 82–84 Via del Babuino),[25] and the Galleria Sangiorgio (in the Palazzo Borghese, Fig. 18). At the last of these, which he visited on 23rd September, he suffered the embarrassment of knocking over a glass and breaking it.

A photographic record of the interior of the Galleria Sangiorgio, crammed with objects (Fig. 19), reveals how easily such an accident might have occurred.[26]

22 Freud's notebook no. 7, fol. 7.16, in: Freud 2021, p. 123.
23 Freud's notebook no. 7, fol. 7.31, in: Freud 2021, p. 128.
24 Illustration from Molnar 1998, p. 40; cf. Müller 2019, p. 185.
25 Freud's notebook no. 7, fol. 7.22, in: Freud 2021, p. 125.
26 Freud's notebook no. 7, fol. 7.32, in Freud 2021, p. 128–29.

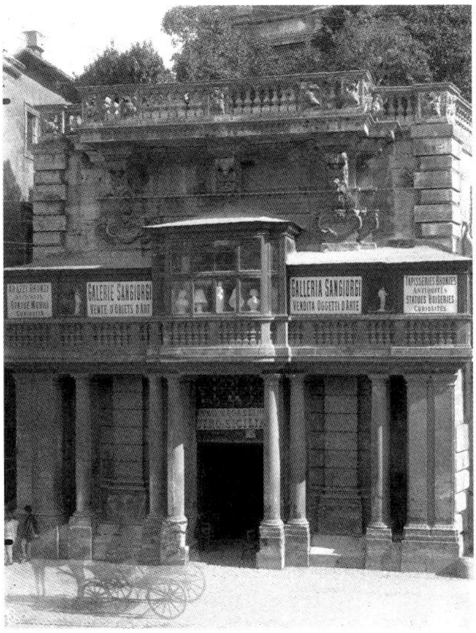

18| Paul Lindner, Galleria Sangiorgio: premises of a dealer in antiquities located within the Palazzo Borghese, Rome. Photograph

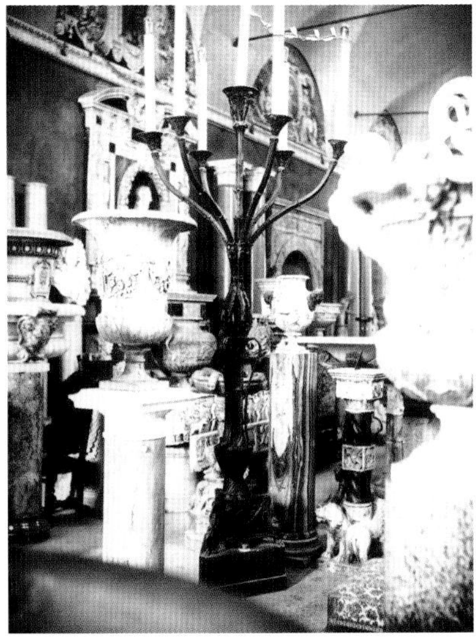

19| Anonymous, View of the interior of the Galleria Sangiorgio, Rome. Photograph

Freud felt, however, that he had been compensated for his misfortune through his discovery, the very next day, at the Musei Vaticani, of the antique relief of the figure known as *Gradiva*, on which he had commented in his essay (published only five months earlier) on the eponymous novella by the poet Wilhelm Jensen.[27] The next entry in his notebook, made on the same day, reveals that this success had led him to the resolution that he should spend more on adding to his collection: "Grand purchases to celebrate my experience and to give me courage in my awareness of being in the gigantic, malevolent city".[28] Freud, it seems, at this time understood the acquisition of works of art as an attempt to keep at bay the city of Rome, which he experienced as overpowering and oppressive. The desired purchases were almost immediately effected, at the gallery of the art dealer Ettore Jandolo (at 92 Via del Babuino).[29] According to Hanns Sachs, the works Freud had by this point acquired were already such as would have impressed those visiting him in Vienna.[30]

27 *SFG*, vol. 11, commentary pp. 13–15.
28 Freud's notebook no. 7, fol. 7.36, in Freud 2021, p. 130.
29 Freud's notebook no. 7, fol. 7.36, in: Freud 2021, p. 130.
30 Sachs 1945, p. 100; Gay 1989, p. 16.

An itemised list of expenditure added, in September 1910, to Freud's notebook reveals that he had made use of a very brief stop in Rome to spend a considerable sum on items for his collection with a further dealer in antiquities, Adriano D'Innocenti (at 77–79 Via del Babuino) and with Knill (at 67 in the same street) and probably also with a number of itinerant dealers.[31]

Upon arriving in Rome in September 1912, Freud immediately drew up a list of the dealers that he wished to visit: yet again, D'Innocenti, then Di Segni, a new name (at 94 Via Condotti), Funaro (at 70 Piazza di Spagna), in addition to the Galleria Sangiorgio, which he had visited in 1907. To these were added all three of the business premises of Ettore Jandolo (in the Via Sistina, the Via Margutta and the Via del Babuino) and, yet again, Knill (also in Via del Babuino).[32] The letter Freud sent to his family on 25th September (with which a note of acquisitions was probably enclosed) reports: "Today I made just a few minor purchases, which will, I hope, be a source of general satisfaction. Rome, in this respect, is even more dangerous than Munich. Every day I wear a gardenia [in my buttonhole] and play at being the rich man, living only for his passions. I'll soon enough have to confront the gravity of the situation. But it was splendid while it lasted".[33]

Acquisitions from south-eastern Europe and through dealers in Berlin

It was by no means only during his travels in Austria and Italy that Freud added to his collection. While at home in Vienna he frequently sought advice by way of an extensive network of those who might be of assistance, be it through up-to-date knowledge of the market or on account of their scholarly expertise. He enjoyed a good deal of support from his colleague Sándor Ferenczi, who maintained his own network of connections among dealers in south-eastern Europe. This region was repeatedly to prove a rich source, with finds frequently excavated by the rural population. On 14th January 1910, for example, Ferenczi sent Freud two figures – a *Hermes* and an *Amor* – both being offered at so modest a price that Freud immediately agreed to buy.[34] In the case of the finds deriving from a supposed former Roman necropolis at Duna-Pentele in Hungary, Freud agreed to Ferenczi's proposal that he be supplied with advance information on what might be about to

31 Freud's notebook no. 9, fol. 9.91, in Freud 2021, p. 208.

32 Freud's notebook no. 10, fols. 10.87 and 10.89, in Freud 2021, pp. 239–40.

33 Letter of 25th September 1912 from Sigmund Freud to Martha Freud, in: *Sigmund Freud* 2003, p. 370.

34 Letters of 14th January 1910 from Sándor Ferenczi to Sigmund Freud, and of 16th January 1910 from Sigmund Freud to Sándor Ferenczi, in: Freud / Ferenczi 1993, p.199.

be unearthed and then offered for sale.[35] Freud was indeed able to make a long series of acquisitions before this mysterious site disappeared.[36]

Freud also acquired a great many works in Berlin. Over the years he made a total of nine visits to the premises of the dealer Philipp Lederer, at 4 Kupfergraben. When awarded the Goethe Prize, in August 1930, Freud spent most of the prize money on acquisitions at Lederer's.[37]

Ludwig Pollak and Emanuel Loewy

Among the scholarly experts who advised Freud as he added to his collection were Ludwig Pollak and Emanuel Loewy, the former an archaeologist, art historian and art dealer, the latter an archaeologist. Pollak, born to a Jewish family in Prague in 1868, had studied in Vienna and, from 1895, had been based in Rome. He first came to wider scholarly attention when, in 1906, he published his research on the discovery of the missing right arm of the *Laocoon*. Thereafter his expertise won the admiration of thousands of scholarly visitors to Rome.[38] In 1915 Pollak was constrained, as an "enemy alien", to leave Italy when it opted to side with the Entente during the First World War. On 16th January 1917 Freud commissioned him to analyse his collection and to prepare an inventory of it (this last was later mislaid). Pollak completed the work in several phases during the course of 1917 and early 1918.[39] Among much else that surprised him, he discovered 89 antique bronze masks that he had himself catalogued, on the occasion of their sale from the collection of the wealthy Roman engineer Prospero Sarti.[40] Meanwhile, Freud and Pollak discovered that they had a strong mutual interest in Johann Wolfgang von Goethe and in Arthur Schopenhauer. On 1st February 1917 they sat up late into the night discussing Freud's article on Michelangelo's *Moses*.[41]

Emanuel Loewy, who was also largely based in Rome, where he had on countless occasions served as a trusted intermediary in the acquisition of antiquities,

35 Letter of 8th February 1910 from Sándor Ferenczi to Sigmund Freud, in: Freud / Ferenczi 1993, p. 210.

36 Letter of 25th February 1910 from Sándor Ferenczi to Sigmund Freud, in: Freud / Ferenczi 1993, p. 220. Cf. Ucko 2001, pp. 298–302; Müller 2019, pp. 191–93. These would now be categorised as finds in informal burial sites (Harmat 1994; Ucko 2001, p. 302).

37 Tögel 2006, pp. 116–18.

38 In 1943 Pollak was deported to Auschwitz, where he was murdered (Merkel Guldan 1988, p. 309). On Pollak, cf. Wolf 1998, p. 69; Jahnke 2018; Rossini 2018b; Trotha 2021 (in the form of a novel).

39 Rossini 2018a, pp. 156–59.

40 Rossini 2018a, pp. 155–56.

41 Rossini 2018a, pp. 157–59.

had been at school with Freud and maintained a close and affectionate relationship with him. It was he, more than anyone, who had first introduced Freud to archaeology.[42]

The experts in Vienna

In Vienna Freud frequently received advice from the art dealers Friedrich Glückselig and Ludwig Lustig, whose premises, at 10 Berggasse, were conveniently close to the Freud family apartment. Between the mid-1920s and 1938 Freud acquired several hundred objects from them.[43] Of particular significance was the role played by the art dealer Otto Fröhlich and his wife, Lili Fröhlich-Bume. Freud's initial contact with them came about through the art historian and psychoanalyst Ernst Kris (who had studied under both Loewy and Freud)[44] and was soon to issue in regular meetings. Writing in 1970 to Karl Eissler, a formerly Viennese psychoanalyst who in 1938 had emigrated to the USA, Lili Fröhlich-Bume recalled:

> "In those days Freud often came to visit us on Sunday mornings, always full of the warmest interest in what we had to show him, and he would acquire a number of the smaller objects, which were to be had for relatively modest sums. He was a true *amateur*, who paid no attention to either the excitement of a chance find or the investment value of an acquisition, but loved the object for its own sake. He was by no means uninformed, but he valued our specialist knowledge, and was much excited by it; he felt convinced that he could trust us to price works fairly, and he never disputed our decisions in this respect. His reason for paying us a visit was often the fee he had recently received for the publication of an article in a foreign journal; as he told us, he liked the idea of using such resources to acquire a new item for the collection. Occasionally, however, we informed him about a piece we had ourselves only just acquired and persuaded him to take a look at it. When he was about to turn 70, we bought a number of items of which he had spoken so as to be able to present these to him to mark the occasion".[45]

42 D'Agata 1994, p. 10; Wolf 1998, pp. 63–67; Rose 2001, pp. 18–19, 64–65; Bergstein 2010, pp. 26–29; O'Donoghue 2019, p. 102.

43 Gamwell 1989, p. 23; D'Agata 1994, p. 11. Cf. *Freud* 1996, p. 161; *Sigmund Freud* 2003, p. 374, note 7; Kogel 2019, p. 70.

44 Rose 2001, pp. 111–33.

45 Letter of 3rd May 1970 from Lili Fröhlich-Bume to Kurt Eissler, here cited after Tögel 2011, p. 58.

Others in Vienna who were able to advise Freud were Hans Demel, from 1926 Keeper of the Egyptian and Middle Eastern Collections at the Kunsthistorisches Museum (of which, two decades later, he became Director), in addition to several others on the curatorial staff at that institution, among them the Keeper of the Collection of Antiquities, Julius Bankó.

The diary that Freud kept between 1929 and 1939 is a mine of information as regards his acquisitions, even if of little more than that. Repeatedly, the entry for any given date consists only of a reference to an item purchased or presented to Freud as a gift. This in itself attests to an interest not only in the collection, but also in its steady growth.[46]

Hans Demel was able to assist Freud one final time during the spring and early summer of 1938. Having arranged a formal valuation of Freud's collection that would, deliberately, estimate this at only 30,000 Reichsmarks (far below its true monetary worth), he was able, on 23rd May, to provide Freud with the related certificate, which would permit the collection to follow him into exile. (Had its estimated value been higher, this would not have been possible.) Freud left Vienna on 4th June and travelled, via Paris, to London.[47]

2. Freud's passion for collecting

During Freud's travels in Italy his pursuit of possible acquisitions for his collection was of no less importance to him than this desire to get to know the cities he visited and the most important works of art and architecture to be found there. In 1917, in the fifth edition of his *Psychopathology of Everyday Life*, Freud commented on this all but unconquerable drive to collect in observing that it had even provoked in him a series of inadvertent mis-readings: "A frustrating, but also laughable, mis-reading to which I am especially prone occurs when I am on holiday and am walking through the streets of a foreign city. It is then invariably the case that I mis-read the signage displayed by any shop that I encounter as 'Antiquities'. In this is manifest the collector's spirit of adventure [*die Abenteuerlust des Sammlers*]".[48]

Scholars have advanced a number of possible reasons for Freud's almost obsessive activity as a collector.[49] There can be no doubt that a significant impulse

46 *Freud* 1996; cf. D'Agata 1994, pp. 9–10; and Davies 1998, pp. 98–99.

47 Gay 1989, pp. 15–16.

48 Freud 1917, p. 79.

49 It has been argued that it was the death of Freud's father that had prompted him to pursue his archaeological interests. Freud's feeling of guilt that his father, on account of his own limited education and his subsequent work commitments, had never been able to do this seemed thereafter to become less dominant (Cassirer Bernfeld 1951, p. 127; Bernfeld &

lay in his desire for a more compelling confirmation – through holding small excavated artefacts in his own hands – of the comparison he had himself drawn between archaeology and psychoanalysis. Freud commented only once on this matter, and not coincidentally at a moment of crisis. On 22nd September 1907, demoralised by a sense of isolation, neglect and despair, he entered in his notebook a summary characterisation of his own grasp of art and art history: "This time the pictures said nothing to me – as for sculpture, I have only ever been able to access what is comprehensible, archaic and original".[50] Implicit here is the belief that Michelangelo's *Moses*, to which Freud had by that date already devoted some thought, remained essentially closed to him. Complex sculptural works of that sort required that one approach them in full possession of the requisite analytical counter-forces. As of September 1907, Freud was not yet able to do that. Affirming that this was so served him as a much-needed form of self-protection.

No less significant here is Freud's reference to what was "comprehensible, archaic and original". The third of these categories – originality – doubtless related, for Freud, to the astonishing presence of those rare works that a collector, in the manner of a hunter, hoped to track down. In this there lay that motivation of his passion for collecting that Freud, in 1917, was to call "the collector's spirit of adventure".[51] The first category – comprehensibility – was here, in all probability, a synonym for simplicity, a quality to which Freud had recently referred in a letter sent from Florence. On account of their prices, Freud had been unable to acquire certain items; by contrast, he did mention "two antique glasses, in coloured glass, adorably simple, and each to be had for *a mere* 200 L".[52]

Of particular importance is the central concept of the three: the "archaic". In his text *The Interest in Psychoanalysis*, Freud was to characterise the "archaic" (in a psychological sense) as a form of regression to childhood experiences that had once been repressed.[53] In an art-historical context, however, the adjective "archaic" does not relate to the symptoms of an illness, but rather to cultural and aesthetic forms that are free of the elaboration occurring during later phases of civilisation. The art works associated with early and indigenous cultures were widely viewed as true witnesses to elemental human energies, of the sort rarely to be

Cassirer Bernfeld 1988, p. 258. For a sceptical view of this argument: Marinelli 1998, p. 11; and Molnar 1998, p. 37). Another explanation sees in Freud's approach to collecting a parallel to his own archiving of dreams, jokes and slips of the tongue (O'Donoghue 2019, p. 112).

50 Freud's notebook no. 7, fol. 7.28, in: Freud 2021, p. 127.

51 Freud 1917, p. 79. See above, p. 49.

52 Letter of 17th September 1907 from Sigmund Freud to his family, in: *Sigmund Freud* 2003, p. 214.

53 Sigmund Freud, "Das Interesse an der Psychoanalyse", in: *SFG*, vol. 13, pp. 219–45, here 239.

found in the conditions of modern civilisation. Such works were seen to offer direct access to that which Freud, in the manner of an archaeologist, sought to extract from the depths of the psyche. In *Totem and Taboo* Freud frequently cited the British anthropologist Edward Burnett Tylor,[54] whose *Primitive Culture*, published in two volumes in 1871 and 1873, had rapidly been translated into German. Tylor had employed the term "survival" to define the enduring validity and relevance of the images of those early cultures such as were to be of interest to Freud.[55] It is no coincidence that the art historian Aby Warburg, who declined an offer of psychoanalysis, nonetheless came close to Freud in his own methods. In May 1907 he wrote to an American colleague that he had in fact devised all the analytical categories he was by then employing in his studies of the Italian Renaissance through reference to what he had learnt from his experience among the "Indians" of New Mexico.[56]

The notebook entry formulated in Freud's sombre mood of September 1907 makes clear that his urge to collect can by no means be dismissed as an eccentric and curious adjunct to the rest of his activity.[57] All the evidence points, rather, to the probability that his collection was integral to his sense of identity. One sign of this lies in the lengths to which Freud would go, well into old age, to ensure that he would be surrounded by items from his collection even in those places where he chose to take his holidays. In May 1930, in connection with his latest acquisitions at Lederer in Berlin, Freud observed: "It's a pity the long holidays are approaching. That means I'll be separated from them".[58] It is clear that the pain of separation was somewhat relieved in the following years. Freud's niece Lilly Freud-Marlé has described how three moving vans were required in order to transport those "things closest to Freud's heart" to his summer residence: "For uncle ought, during his hard-earned vacation, to be surrounded by everything that had become dear to him and familiar to him. But oh! – the chaos these things caused before each one had found its appointed place".[59]

54 Sigmund Freud, "Über einige Übereinstimmungen im Seelenleben der Wilden und der Neurotiker", in: *SFG*, vol. 13, pp. 11–100, here 13. For further instances, see that volume's index, p. 423. On Tylor as a source of great interest to Freud: Barth 2013, p, 33.

55 Tylor (German translation) 1873. Cf. Didi-Huberman 2002b (English translation); and Didi-Huberman 2010 (German translation), pp. 58–67.

56 Letter of 17th May 1907 from Aby Warburg to James Mooney, in: Warburg 2001, vol. VI.1, no. 325, p. 328; cf. Bredekamp 2019, p. 99.

57 See above, pp. 9–10.

58 Letter of 12th May 1930 from Sigmund Freud to Martha Freud, here cited after: Tögel 2006, p. 118.

59 Freud-Marlé 2006, pp. 67–68. Cf. Tögel 2015, p. 76.

The probability that this account relates to a substantial part of Freud's collection is suggested by the description provided by a visitor to Freud on holiday, in June 1935, at 47 Strassergasse in the Viennese suburb of Grinzing:

> "Before I sat down I looked briefly around the room, and the first thing I noticed was that there were a great many small tables [...] and glazed display cabinets, all of which were filled with small antique objects. On his desk there were papers and a few books. Yet far greater in number, here too, were small antiquities. On the table there were several trays, each tightly packed with figures and images. It looked just like a room in a museum for 'small works of art' – there were so many small sculptures and figures".[60]

Ernest Jones reports that Freud esteem for the collection appeared to be even greater when he was on holiday, in as far as he made a point of ritually greeting newly acquired pieces when the family gathered for lunch. According to Jones, it was Freud's habit to bring each new antique acquisition, "usually a small statuette", to the lunch table, where, during the course of the meal, it would stand in front of his place. When lunch was over it would be returned to his desk; but it would thereafter reappear several times on the table.[61] The placing of such figures in front of the head of the household, as also the repetition of this procedure, must have had a ceremonial character, which would in turn have given the family meal a special stamp. It would, at least, have been a compensation for the fact that items from the collection would, in due course, be on display only in Freud's consulting room and study at 19 Berggasse.

Such traditions testify to the fact that Freud retained, to the very end of his life, that close relationship to the items in his collection, of which he first spoke during the summer of 1899.[62] Without his collection, Freud would not have been fully himself. It was the product of his own passions and efforts and was closely related to his experience of travel and the great expeditions he conducted in the realm of ideas; and it served as a source of inspiration for his psychoanalytic research. But that was not all. As installed in his consulting room and study at 19 Berggasse, the collection was to become a means of communication with those who visited him there, be they colleagues or patients; and it is to this role that is owed its importance in the context of psychoanalysis.

60 Here cited after the translation in: Tögel 2015, pp. 75–76.

61 Jones 1957, p. 438.

62 Letter of 1st August 1899 from Sigmund Freud to Wilhelm Fliess, in: Freud / Fliess 1986, p. 399. See above, p. XI.

3. Images as a living ambience

The installation at 19 Berggasse

The character of the spacious Freud family apartment on the first floor at 19 Berggasse was marked by the visual contrast between, on the one hand, the living quarters used by all and the waiting room intended for use by Freud's patients and, on the other, the two spaces which equated to Freud's own domain: his consulting room and his study. The ground plan (Fig. 20) shows how those calling on Freud in his professional capacity would ascend the steps, be admitted to the lobby of the waiting room and, from there, be able to access the waiting room itself. Here, there was no object that might detract from an impression that one was in a perfectly ordinary domestic space. How striking a contrast would then have been experienced by any first-time visitor as he left the waiting room to enter the adjacent consulting room, from which he would have been able also to glimpse, through doors invariably left open, the study that lay beyond it.

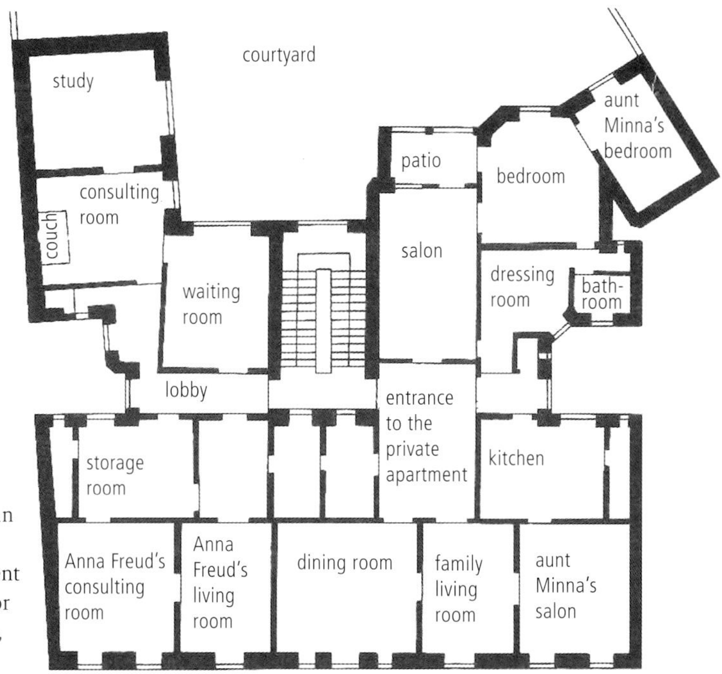

20| Ground plan of the Freud family apartment on the first floor at 19 Berggasse, Vienna

In both of these spaces the focus was entirely, and unmistakably, upon an encounter with the display of items from Freud's collection, its impact further heightened through the presence of the numerous photographs and reproductions of works of art that covered the walls, and (in the study) the enveloping

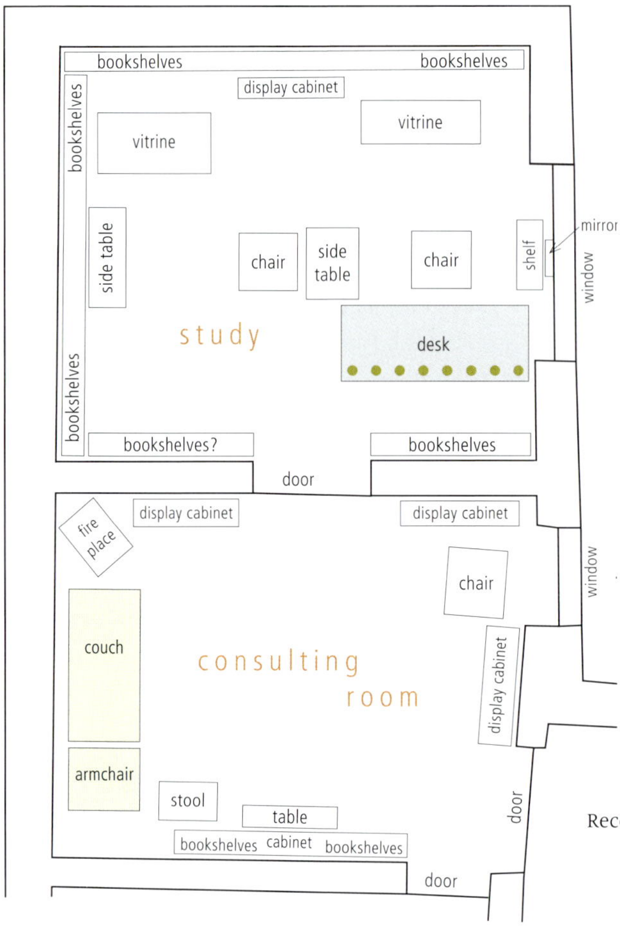

21| Marie Egger, Reconstruction of Freud's consulting room and study at 19 Berggasse, Vienna: ground plan, furnishing

presence of floor-to-ceiling bookshelves. While there is here no scope for a comprehensive description and analysis of these two interiors, a summary tour of each will here suffice to elucidate what was so extraordinary about these caves of imagery. We are here indebted to the photographic record of the entire apartment at 19 Berggasse that was made by Edmund Engelman in May 1938, in order to preserve an image of the site of the founding of psychoanalysis before Freud and his family (with no option but to emigrate) left Vienna for London.[63] These photographs allow one to establish at least an approximate sense of the appearance, arrangement and contents of the consulting room and of the study (Fig. 21).

63 Engelman 1977a.

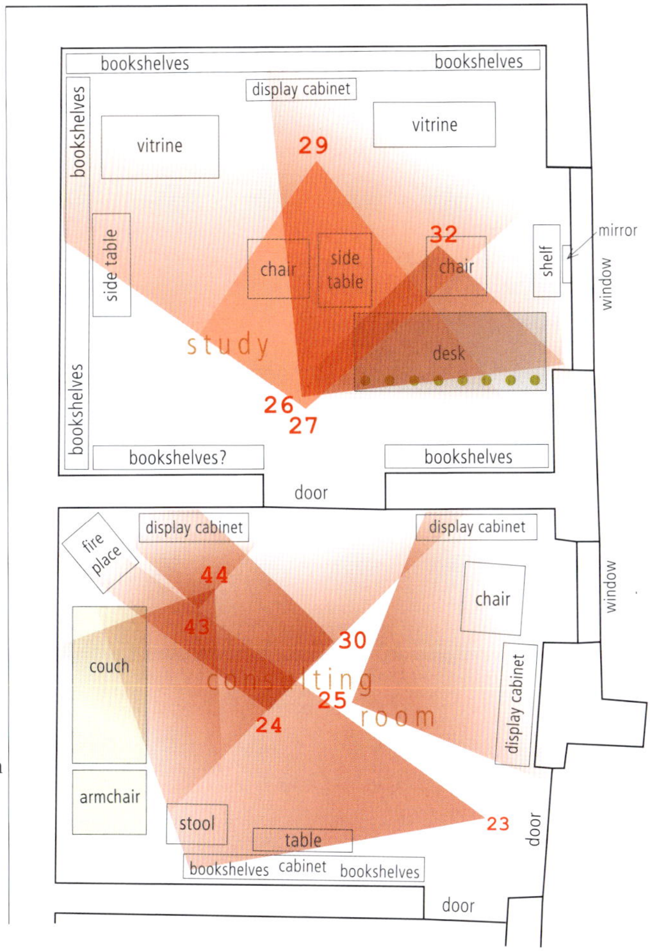

22| Marie Egger, Reconstruction of Freud's consulting room and study at 19 Berggasse, Vienna: ground plan with projected position of Engelman's camera taking photographs here illustrated as Figs. 23–32, 42–44

Engelman's photographs (those reproduced here, as Figs. 23–32 and 42–44, are keyed, in each case, to the adjacent ground plan; see also Fig. 22) record Freud's collection in its final state. But the earliest surviving accounts of it, which come from Hanns Sachs and Ludwig Binswanger in 1912 and 1914, already approximate the visual impression captured around 25 years later.[64]

Upon advancing from the waiting room to the consulting room, and then entering that space for the first time, the prospective analysand would come upon an emphatically furnished interior that surely defied his expectations, above all because a space in which imagination might be expected to unfurl and take flight was to a large extent already so densely defined through the presence

64 See below, pp.74–75.

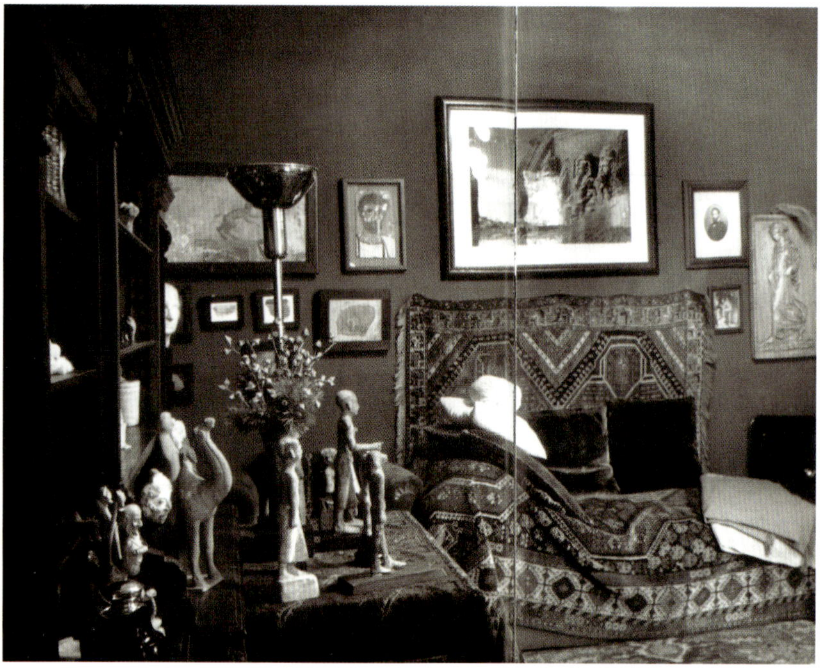

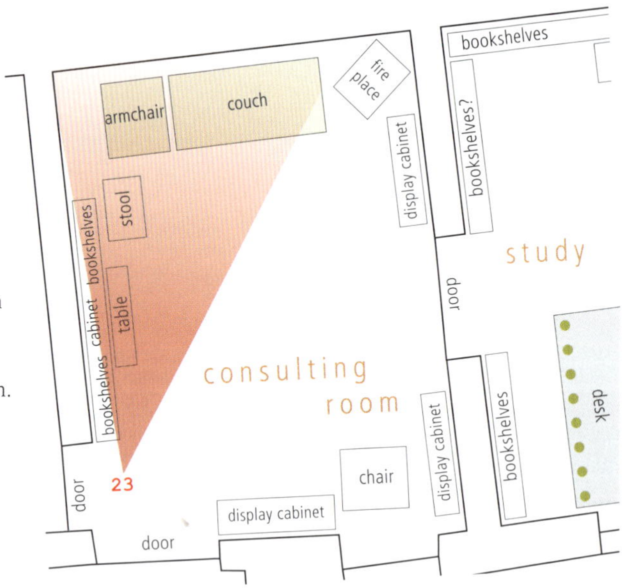

23| Edmund Engelman, View upon entering the consulting room from the adjacent waiting room. Directly opposite, against the far wall: the couch. May 1938. Photograph

of books, images and sculpted figures (Fig. 23). Along the wall to his immediate left he would find bookshelves flanking a large, centrally positioned cabinet, in which sculptural items were displayed, while directly in front of this was a table on which there stood a number of statuettes.

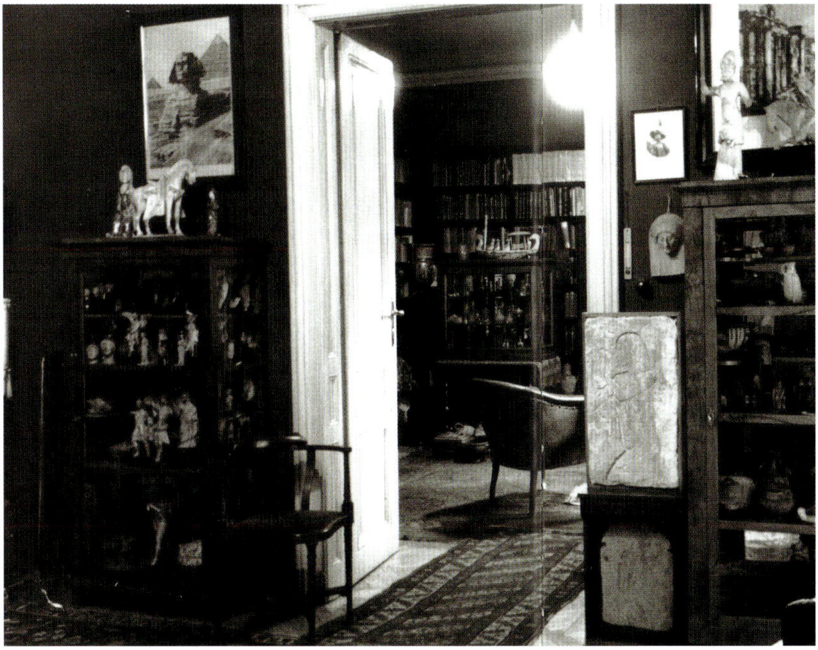

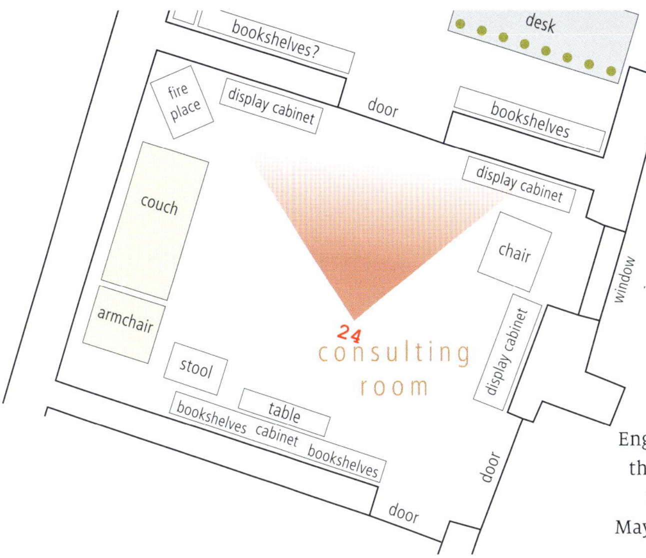

24| Edmund Engelman, View from the consulting room towards the study. May 1938. Photograph

The wall directly opposite was dominated by the presence of the couch. This was, however, accompanied by a veritable "gallery" of images: reproductions of works of art and photographic records of sites visited during Freud's travels. Turning to the right, the new arrival would discover a set of double doors flanked by two glazed, densely packed display cabinets and, were the doors open (which was invariably the case), a view into Freud's study (Fig. 24).

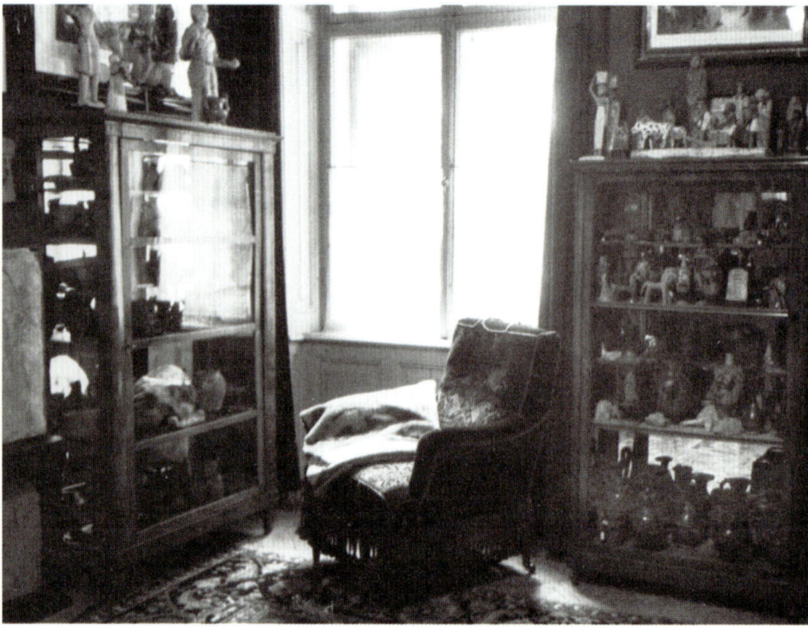

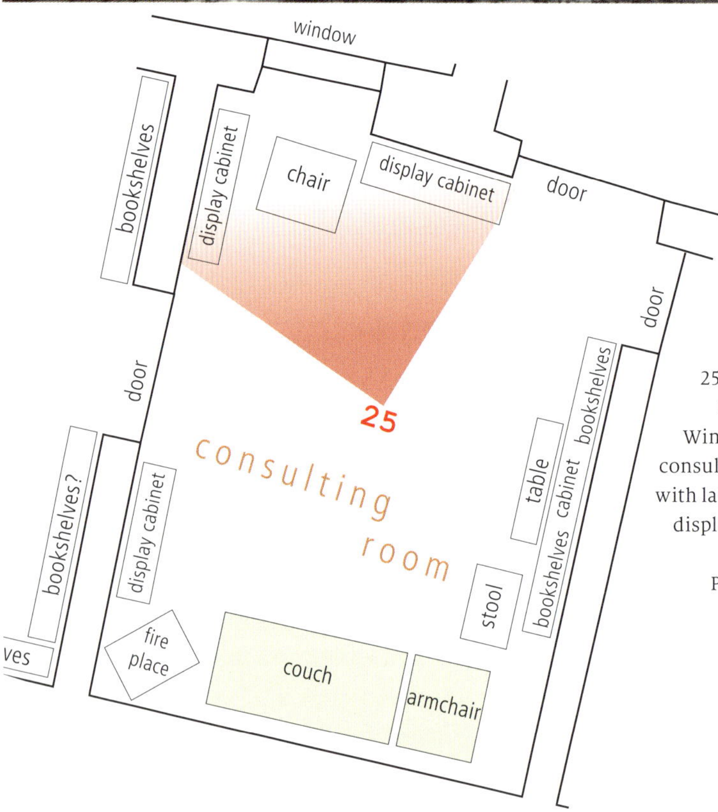

25| Edmund Engelman, Window of the consulting room, with large, glazed display cabinet. May 1938. Photograph

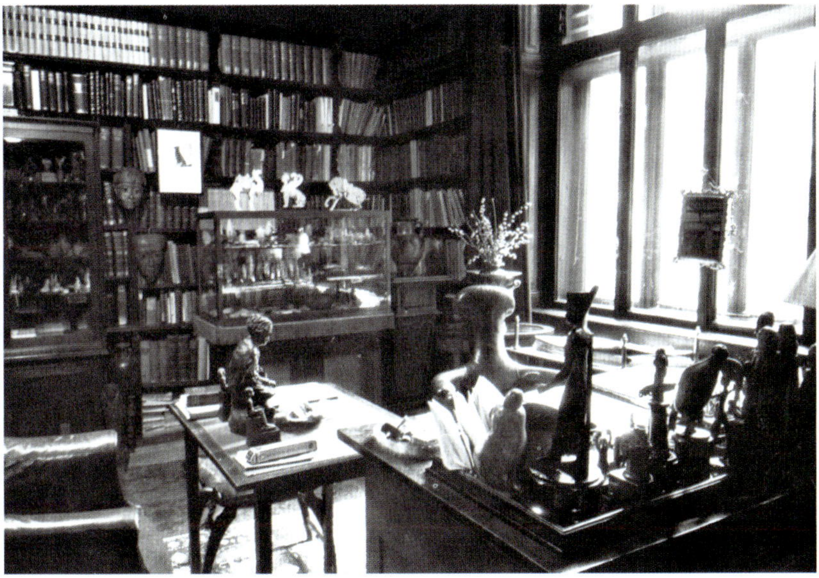

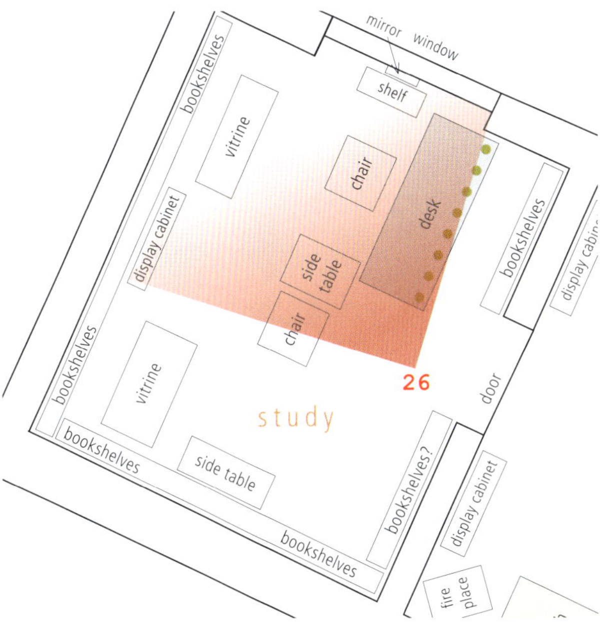

26| Edmund Engelman, Freud's study, with desk, large window and one of several walls of bookshelves. May 1938. Photograph

Remaining in the consulting room, but turning further to the right, he would discover a window and a large, glazed cabinet in which statuettes were displayed (Fig. 25). Passing from the consulting room into the study, he would immediately grasp that this space was no less well fitted to display items from the collection (Fig. 26).

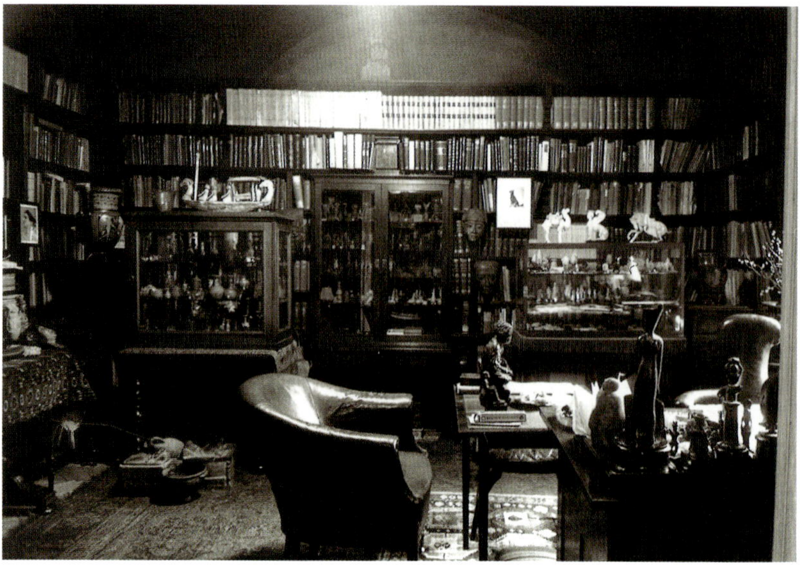

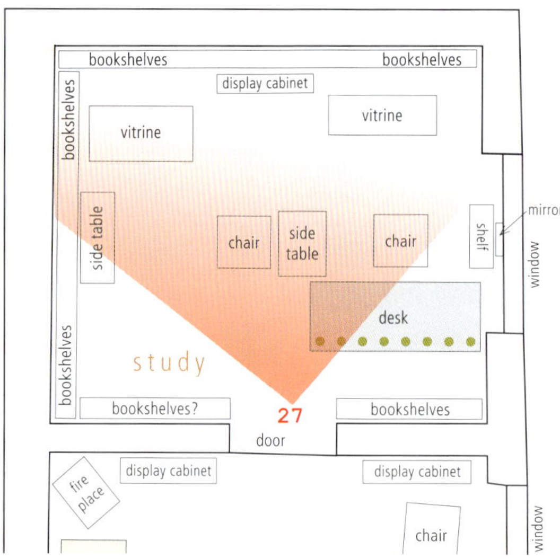

27| Edmund Engelman, Freud's study, with view of wall of bookshelves, centrally positioned large display cabinet and two free-standing vitrines. May 1938. Photograph

Here, to the right of the entrance, was a desk, along the rear surface of which stood numerous small, sculpted figures. To the left was a side table in addition to a chair for visitors. Light entered from the right through a large window, where there was also to be found a mirror.[65] The wall directly facing the entrance to the study (Fig. 27) comprised shelving intended chiefly for books, although small

65 *Freud, Berggasse 19* 2020, pp. 218–19. On the motif of the mirror in Freud and Lacan: Fuss 2004, pp. 83–87.

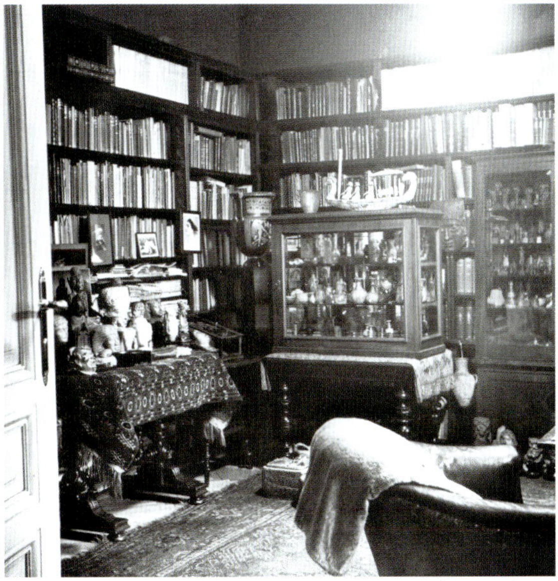

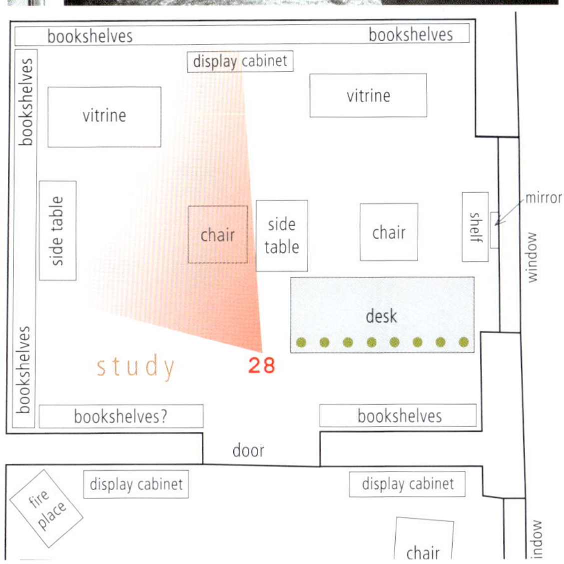

28| Edmund Engelman, A corner of Freud's study with bookshelves and one of two free-standing vitrines. May 1938. Photograph

works of art and diverse objects might also be found there, among the latter two masks from Egyptian mummies. At the centre of this wall stood a further large display cabinet. There were, in addition, two free-standing vitrines, each displaying small sculpted figures.

The wall of Freud's study that lay opposite the window (to which, it appears, Engelman did not devote a separate photograph) was made up entirely of bookshelves; but further statuettes and objects were displayed on the small side table positioned in front of it, as also in the free-standing vitrine (Fig. 28). The view of

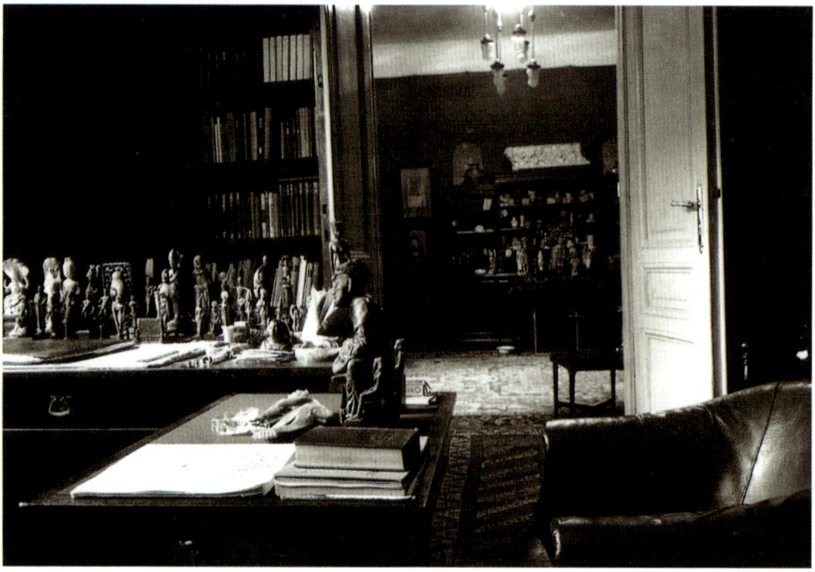

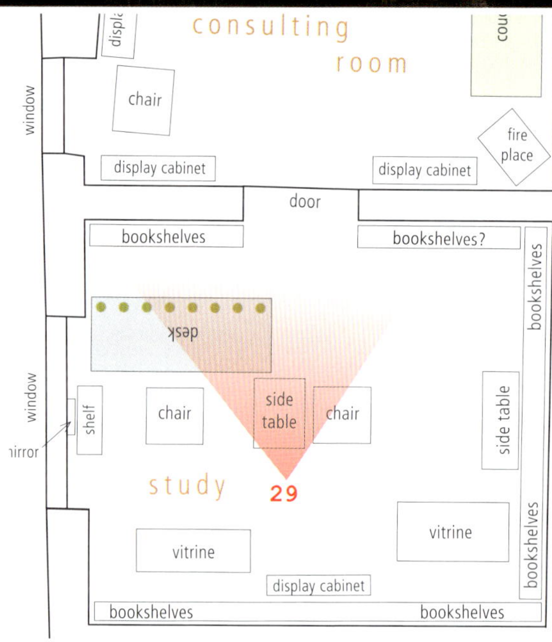

29| Edmund Engelman, View from the visitor's chair: desk and bookshelves in Freud's study, with the consulting room beyond. May 1938. Photograph

the study from the visitor's chair (Fig. 29) encompassed the alignment of sculpted figures along the far edge of the desk, the bookshelves behind this and, in the consulting room beyond, a large cabinet on the far wall and the table in front of this. As these photographs indisputably reveal, in neither the consulting room nor in Freud's study was there any chance to evade the impression of this theatre of sculptural imagery.

The wall with the couch

Within this ensemble two pieces of furniture merit particular attention: in the consulting room the couch, and in the study the desk. Among Engelman's photographs of May 1938, one of those that has now come to attract considerable scholarly interest shows how the legendary couch (a gift to Freud from a former patient, Josephine Benevisti) was accompanied by images that have an evident connection with psychoanalysis (Fig. 30).[66]

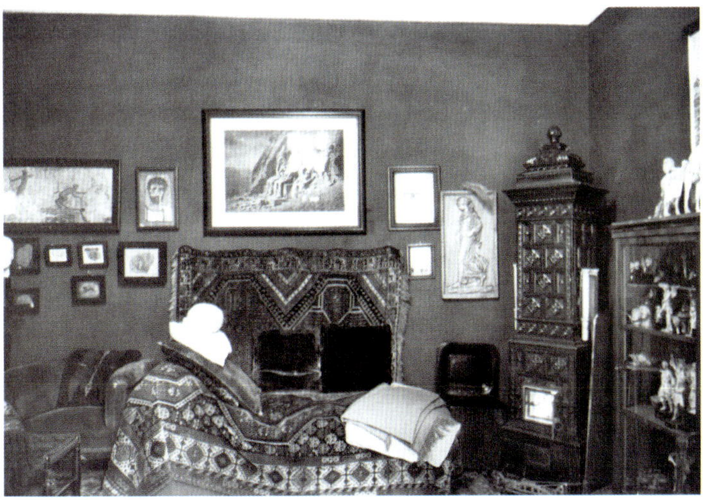

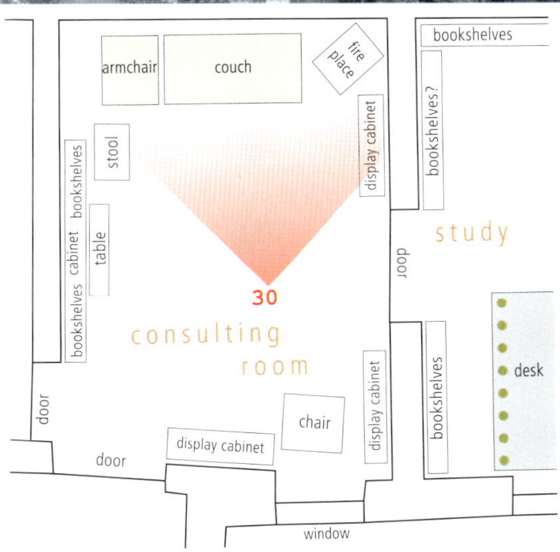

30| Edmund Engelman, Consulting room, with couch and images displayed across the wall behind it. May 1938. Photograph

66 On the couch: Marinelli 2006, pp. 23–24; also Tögel 2017, and Guderian 2018, with a fundamental characterisation of the space of the consulting room as a determining factor in the relationship between analyst and analysand.

At the upper left, above the armchair in which Freud had, since 1924, generally sat while his patient lay on the couch, two fragments of wall painting from Pompeii attest to his great interest in the campaigns of excavation at that site, which he regarded as synonymous with the role of psychoanalysis in relation to the unconscious.[67] Above the couch itself hung an image of the huge rock temple at Abu Simbel, erected by Ramesses II in Egyptian Nubia. Its presence was possibly intended as a reference to Freud's conviction that Moses had been born in Egypt, a matter he would seek to reinterpret in *Moses and Monotheism*.[68]

To the right of the couch there hung a plaster cast of a relief from Antiquity known as *Gradiva* (Fig. 31), which in 1902 had served the poet Wilhelm Jensen as the starting point for his eponymous novella.[69] This is the story of an archaeologist to whom the depicted woman appeared to be real. He became convinced that he was succumbing to madness until he recognised that the impression of encountering, in the relief, a real person derived from the physical resemblance between the depicted woman and a friend from his childhood. The archaeologist falls in love with the latter and at length asks her to marry him. For Freud, this narrative was most instructive concerning the fragments of the unconscious that derived from childhood and yet persisted into adulthood as if dreamily leading a life of their own. In his analysis of Jensen's novella, published in May 1907 as *Delusion and Dream in Jensen's "Gradiva"*,[70] Freud emphasised the structural resemblance between archaeology and psychoanalysis (a theme to which he would return three decades later): "There is really no better analogy for the repression that makes an aspect of the mind inaccessible, even while preserving it, than the burial that was the fate of Pompeii, on account of which, through the wielding of many spades, that city could be restored".[71]

One of the very few moments of happiness during Freud's crisis-ridden stay in Rome of September 1907 occurred, as mentioned earlier, when he came upon what he took to be the original *Gradiva* relief in the Musei Vaticani: "Discovered Gradiva XXVII 644 Collezione Chiaramonti 24.9.07: overjoyed to have seen some-

67 He had acquired at least one of the displayed images by the spring of 1909. (I am grateful to Christfried Tögel for this information.)

68 Gamwell 1989, pp. 25–26, sees here a symbol of the father.

69 Jensen 1973. From the extensive literature on Freud's engagement with this novella, of particular note are: Rose 2001, pp. 89–96; Bergstein 2010, pp. 115–35, 182–84; Mayer 2011; Kogel 2019, pp. 188–94; Müller 2019, pp. 208–15.

70 Sigmund Freud, "Der Wahn und die Träume in W. Jensens 'Gradiva'", in *SFG*, vol. 11, pp. 13–88.

71 Sigmund Freud, "Der Wahn und die Träume in W. Jensens 'Gradiva'", in: *SFG*, vol. 11, p. 45. Cf. Mayer 2011.

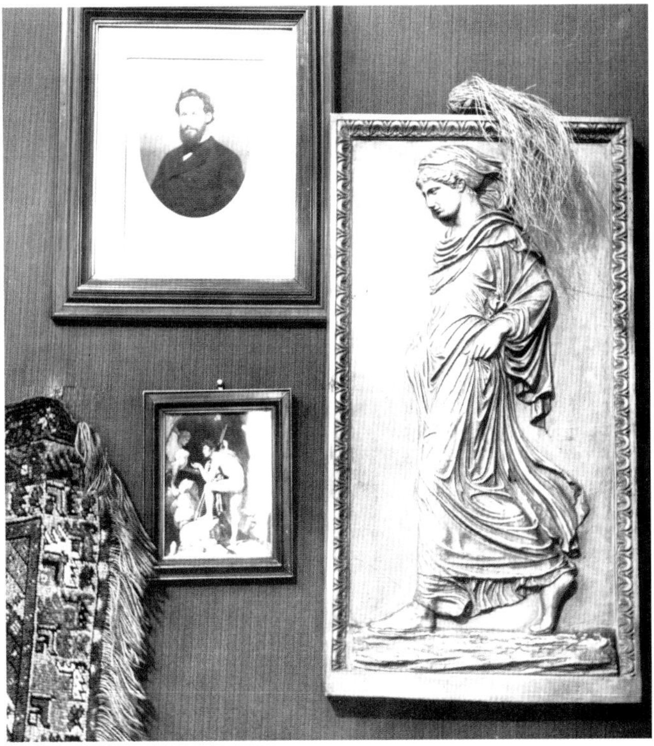

31| Edmund Engelman, Images displayed on the wall beyond the foot of the couch: plaster cast of relief of *Gradiva* (right), and small reproduction of Ingres' *Oedipus with the Sphinx* (lower left). May 1938. Photograph

thing I knew".[72] Freud later learnt that the supposedly Roman figure described in Jensen's novella derived in fact from a Greek original.[73] The cast of the relief of *Gradiva* that hung in Freud's consulting room[74] was thus dense with meaning for him, in addition to being yet another compelling instance of the interconnection between art, dreams and the work of psychoanalysis.

72 Freud's notebook no. 7, fol. 7.35, in: Freud 2021, p. 130.

73 Sigmund Freud, "Der Wahn und die Träume in W. Jensens 'Gradiva'", in: *SFG*, vol. 11, p. 15.

74 This may have been the cast that Karl Abraham gave Freud in December 1908 (letter of 18th December 1908 from Karl Abraham to Sigmund Freud, in: Freud / Abraham 1980, p. 71; cf. letter of 26th December 1908 from Sigmund Freud to Karl Abraham, in: Freud / Abraham 1980, p. 71) or another, which Freud acquired from its producer in Munich. (I am grateful to Christfried Tögel for this information.)

A dried papyrus plant, tucked between the wall and the frame of the cast, with its fronds tumbling over the subject's head and shoulders, intensifies the personal connection with Freud. He had probably picked this himself during his stay in Syracuse in September 1910,[75] and it meant a great deal to him. Paula Fichtl, the housekeeper at 19 Berggasse, would ask those patients visiting Freud for the first time to take care as they reclined upon the couch, for the papyrus, if touched, would instantly crumble to dust.[76]

Between the couch and the relief of *Gradiva* there hung a small reproduction of an early-19th-century painting that Freud had first come to know in the mid-1880s in Paris: *Oedipus with the Sphinx* by Jean-Auguste-Dominique Ingres. Freud had always seen Oedipus, the solver of riddles, as an allegory of his own studies and thus also of himself. And the numerous sphinxes to be found in his collection also support zhat view. Behind his desk there was the sculpture of a sphinx;[77] and this was a hint not lost on his pupils. For his 50th birthday, on 6th May 1906, at the suggestion of the psychoanalyst Paul Federn (one of Freud's first pupils), they commissioned a medallion from the Viennese sculptor Carl Maria Schwerdtner. The obverse bore a profile portrait of Freud, while the reverse showed a sphinx, no less physically powerful than chillingly malevolent. Facing the sphinx was Oedipus, shown reflectively leaning upon his staff, as if untroubled in confronting the monster.[78] To the right, and behind the figure of Oedipus, appeared an inscription in Greek: "He solved the famous riddle and was indeed a powerful man", a quotation from Sophocles' *Oedipus Rex*, a text treasured by Freud since his schooldays. As a young student he had dreamt of being immortalised with those words. When that actually happened, he felt almost awkward.[79]

The desk

The desk to be found in Freud's study may be recognised as the effective engine room of intellectual inspiration. In its most distinctive characteristic, it did not in fact serve Freud exclusively as a desk in the strict sense of that term but, rather, as a further, and especially privileged, site for the display of items from his collection.

75 Letter of 2nd October 1910 from Sigmund Freud to Sándor Ferenczi, in: Freud 1968, p. 297.

76 Cassirer Bernfeld 1951, p. 110.

77 Tögel 2013, pp. 14–19.

78 Galst & van Alfen 2013, cat. IV.261, p. 240. The medallion was cast in both silver and bronze.

79 Armstrong, Leonard & Orrells 2023, pp. 9–19, here 16; cf. Alt 2016, pp. 53–54. The cited words are from Sophocles' *Oedipus Rex*, l. 1525.

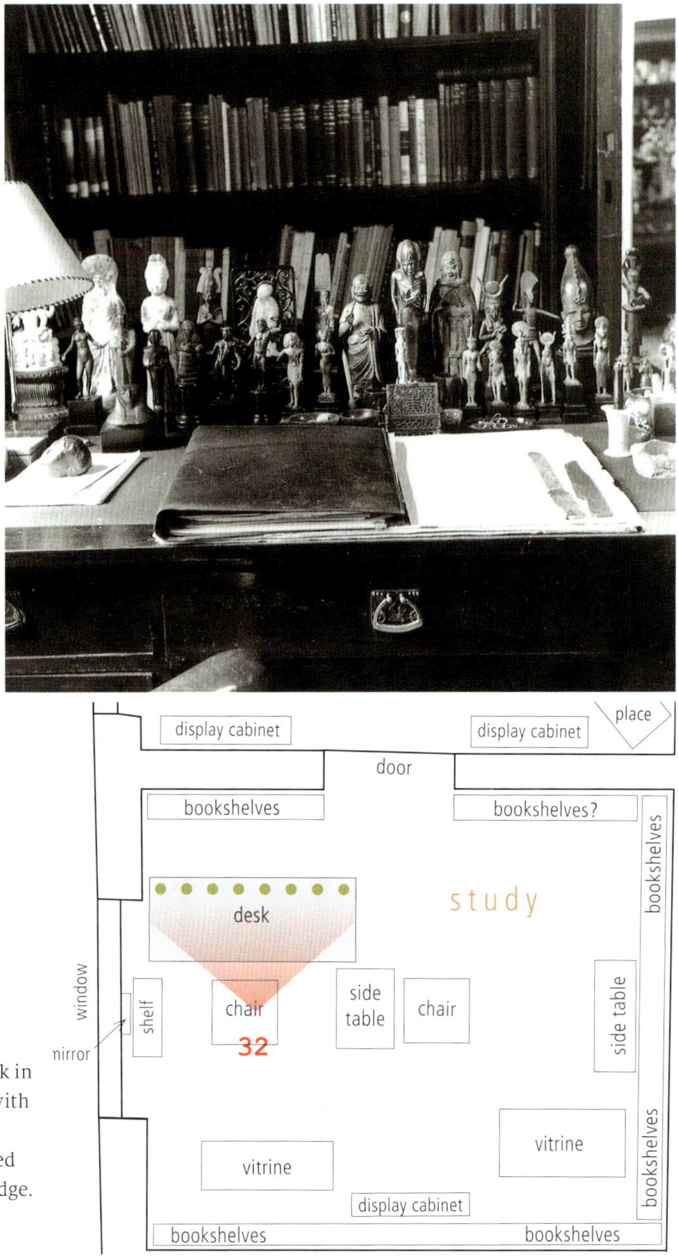

32| Edmund Engelman, Desk in Freud's study with figures, facing inwards, aligned along its rear edge. May 1938. Photograph

While the entire rear edge of the surface of the desk was reserved for these, both their disposition (facing inwards) and their arrangement (aligned in the manner of a palisade, Fig. 32) are indications that, unlike most of the collection, their chief, if by no means only, addressee was Freud himself.

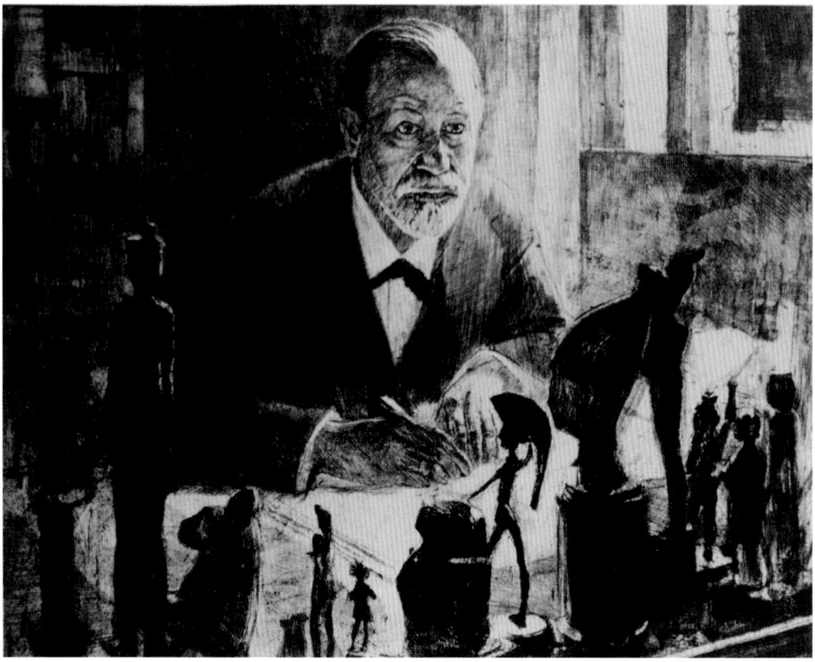

33| Max Pollak, *Portrait of Sigmund Freud*, 1914. Etching. London, Freud Museum

Of particular interest in this context is the portrait of Freud made by Max Pollak (Fig. 33). As mentioned earlier, Pollak had made the drawings that accompanied Freud's article on Michelangelo's *Moses*;[80] and he had been present when the decision was taken, in February 1914, to publish that text in the journal *Imago*. It was at around this time that he made the etching, which shows Freud seated at his desk in the company of items from his collection in their great diversity of shapes and sizes.[81]

Between the daylight entering through the window to the right and the Rembrandtian darkness encroaching from the left, Freud sits, with pen in hand, but with his focused, eager face momentarily raised, as if gathering thoughts or summoning inspiration. Responding to the image on 6th March, Sándor Ferenczi termed it "*outstanding* [...] the etcher is apparently not a 'modernist', but one detects the thinner air [of modernism] in his work".[82] On 28th March Karl Kraus, in his own Viennese journal, *Die Fackel*, could not resist the corrosive wit of quoting

80 See above, p. 29–30.

81 *Allgemeines Lexikon der bildenden Künstler*, vol. 27, p. 216.

82 Letter of 6th March 1914 from Sándor Ferenczi to Sigmund Freud, in: Freud / Ferenczi 1993, p. 290.

lines from the dedication to Goethe's *Faust* that referred to "smoke and fog", but went on to emphasise how successful Pollak had been in seeking to convey the nature of "focused intellectual and creative work through the motif of the inwardly directed gaze".[83] On 2nd April Karl Abraham told Freud: "A few days ago Pollak's etching arrived. What I like most of all is that he has so captured the way you sit.

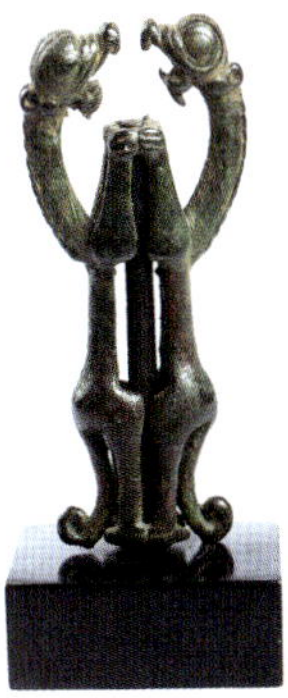
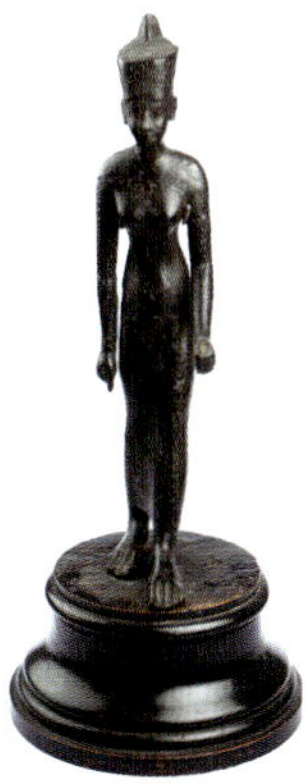
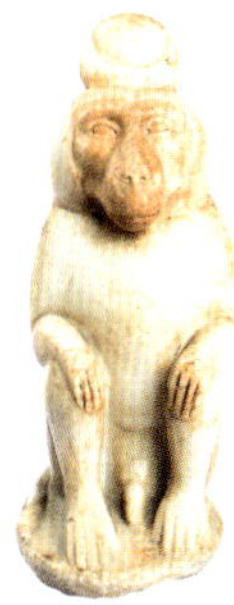
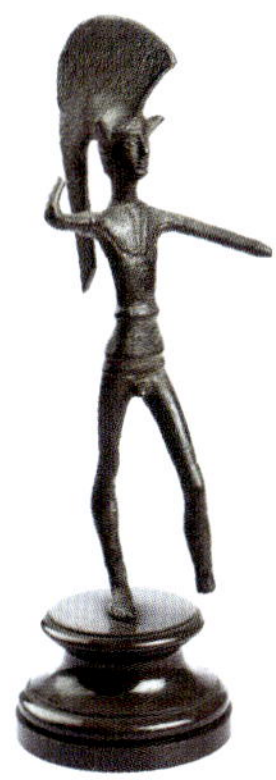

34| Holder for a banner with symmetrically positioned spitting wildcats, western Iran, c. 800 BC. Bronze. London, Freud Museum, no. 3043 —— 35| Statuette of Neith, Egypt, Late Period. Bronze. London, Freud Museum, no. 3134 —— 36| Thot in his incarnation as a baboon, Egyptian, Roman Period. Marble. London, Freud Museum, no. 3133 —— 37| Etruscan warrior, c. 500–450 BC. Bronze. London, Freud Museum, no. 3135

This, one grasps immediately; whereas the facial expression requires some time to make out. But then one recognises how good that is, too. The execution as a whole, especially the distribution of black and white, is most accomplished".[84]

In keeping with the emphasis, throughout the image, on the contrast between light and dark, the diverse figures from the collection are set off against the surface of the desk as sharply outlined silhouettes. In most cases this permits identification. At the extreme left, where a degree of guess-work is required, it appears that Pollak has recorded the presence of a work of around 800 BC that Freud had acquired with the help of Ferenczi: an Iranian bronze holder for a banner, with symmetrically positioned figures of spitting wildcats (Fig. 34).[85] The neighbouring, much smaller figure is a Late Egyptian bronze statuette of Neith, goddess of

83 Kraus 1914.

84 Letter of 2nd April 1914 from Karl Abraham to Sigmund Freud, in: Freud / Abraham 1980, p. 166.

85 Spankie 2019, cat. 7, p. 30.

hunting and of war, but also protectress of both the living and the dead. She wears a crown and an ankle-length gown (Fig. 35).[86] To her right stands the compact figure of the Egyptian god of intellectual endeavour and, above all, of writing: Thot, here in his incarnation as a baboon (Fig. 36).[87]

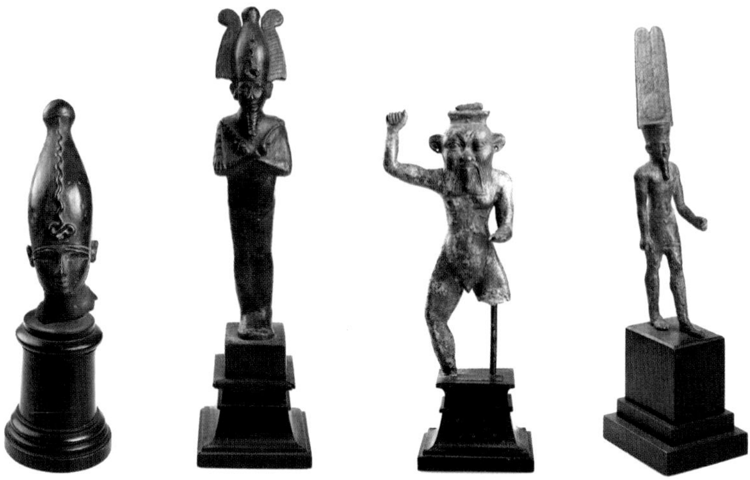

38| Head of Osiris, c. 850 BC. Bronze. London, Freud Museum, no. 3128 ___ 39| Statuette of Osiris, Egypt, Late Period. Copper alloy. London, Freud Museum, no. 3136 ___ 40| Bes, god of the home and the family, Egyptian, c. 600 BC. Bronze. London, Freud Museum, no. 3485 ___ 41| Statuette of Amon-Re, Egyptian, 716–332 BC. Bronze. London, Freud Museum, no. 3138

To the right of three small figure that cannot be identified is to be found yet another example of the Egyptian god Thot, its positioning here, in such proximity to Freud's writing hand, doubtless intended to acknowledge, and perhaps to invoke, its supernatural capacity. To its right stands the stylised figure of an Etruscan warrior (Fig. 37), which Freud may well have acquired from Riccardo Mancini during one of his visits to Orvieto.[88] The large head is that of Osiris (Fig 38): god of life, of death, of the Underworld and, notably, of transformation. This item was evidently a particular source of inspiration in Freud's approach to

86 *Freud's Sculpture* 2006, p. 40; Spankie 2019, cat. 1, p. 18.

87 *Sigmund Freud and Art*, 1989, pp. 56–57; *"Meine ... alten und dreckigen Götter"* 1998, cat. 11, pp. 111–12; *Freud's Sculpture* 2006, p. 45; Spankie 2019, cat. 16, p. 48.

88 *Sigmund Freud and Art* 1989, p. 106; *"Meine ... alten und dreckigen Götter"* 1998, cat. 68, p. 138; Spankie 2019, cat. 6, p. 28.

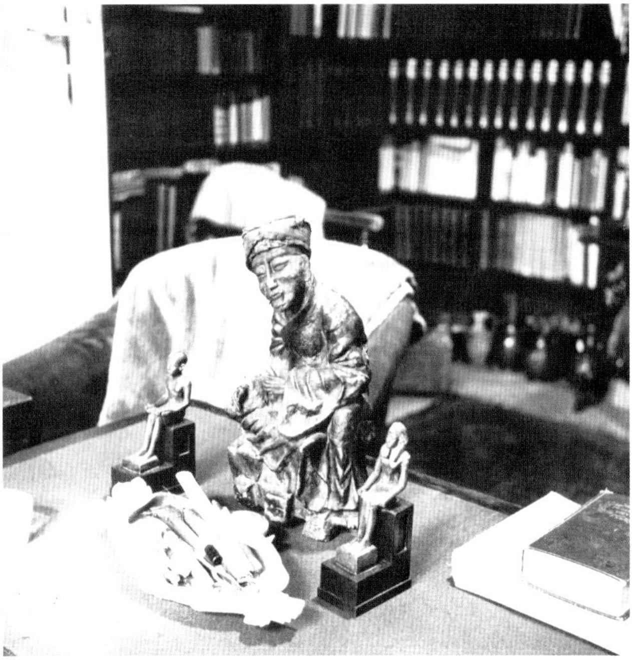

42| Edmund Engelman, Side table in Freud's study with large, seated Chinese figure representing a Taoist scholar, flanked by two small enthroned Egyptian deities. May 1938. Photograph

analysis.[89] The head is here accompanied by a tall figural variant of the same deity, positioned almost directly opposite Freud (Fig. 39).

The small figure with its arm raised is evidently also an Egyptian statuette. In this case the deity represented is Bes: protector of the home and of the family (Fig. 40).[90] The penultimate item of those visible here might perhaps be a reduced version of a figure of the divine Osiris. A series of figures from Egypt would, however, be incomplete without the addition of Amon-Re, who is present at the extreme right, posed as if sturdily stepping forward (Fig. 41).[91] In marked contrast to the darkness of all the other figures, Pollak's rendering of Amon-Re with his magnificent head-gear – a gleaming tuft of feathers clasping a solar disc – is a bright form set against a darker background.

89 Spankie 2019, cat. 19, p. 116. Cf. Davies 1998, pp. 97–98; and *Freud's Sculpture* 2006, p. 41; Spankie 2019, cat. 9, p. 34.

90 *Freud as Collector* 1996, cat. 25, p. 32.

91 *Sigmund Freud and Art* 1989, pp. 46–47; *"Meine … alten und dreckigen Götter"* 1998, no. 24, p. 118; *Freud's Sculpture* 2006, p. 43; Spankie 2019, cat. 12, p. 40.

The identity of the divinities and other figures depicted in Pollak's etching draws attention to Freud's particular interest in Ancient Egypt, which was to find further confirmation in his aforementioned volume of 1939, *Moses and Monotheism*.[92] But in fact all the items in Freud's collection, whatever their original geo-cultural context, served him as a source of the inspiration he drew from archaeology as a model for psychoanalysis and from his personal encounters, while in Italy, of excavations in progress.

Engelman's photographs of the study in fact began with those objects that stood on the side table, their arrangement not unlike that of an altar (Fig. 42):[93] a large, seated Chinese figure representing a Taoist scholar, flanked by two small Egyptian deities, one of them Imhotep, god of knowledge and medicine. When Engelman took his photographs, in May 1938, several items intruded upon the view of these: a shallow oval dish containing writing implements and a stack of manuscript pages held in place by an English dictionary. Freud made a point of greeting the Taoist scholar every morning.[94]

Objects and analysis

Although there was a distinct emphasis, within Freud's collection, on figures from Ancient Egypt, its display was unsystematic. And this was true of every aspect of the way in which the items were installed at 19 Berggasse. The photograph of the wall with the couch in the consulting room (see Fig. 30) shows, at its right extremity, one of the many glazed display cabinets with a dense accumulation of small, sculpted forms both inside and on top of it. A frontal view of this cabinet, such as would be obtained by an analysand reclining on the couch (Fig. 43),[95] at first gives the impression that the objects were here arranged with no regard to any archaeological or art-historical system.

Freud's own interests would lead one to suppose that he would have displayed such objects so as to reflect cultural or chronological considerations. But, according to the advice that he had himself provided, in 1912, in his "Recommendations to Physicians Practising Psycho-Analysis", the application of every logic

92 Sigmund Freud, "Der Mann Moses und die monotheistische Religion", in *SFG*, vol. 20, pp. 223–347. Cf. Handler Spitz 1989, pp. 155–59; and Marinelli 1998, pp. 16–17. The analysis of Joan Raphael-Leff (1990) suggests that Freud's great interest in Egyptian figures and the culture of Ancient Egypt in general, by contrast with his relative lack of interest in the related mythology, may have been connected with the traumas of his own childhood.

93 Engelman 1977a, fig. 26 and p. 144; Spankie 2019, cat. 18, p. 52.

94 Spector 1972, p. 15. Cf. Gamwell 1989, pp. 27 and 32, note 36. The Chinese figure was probably not old.

95 Engelman 1977a, p. 47.

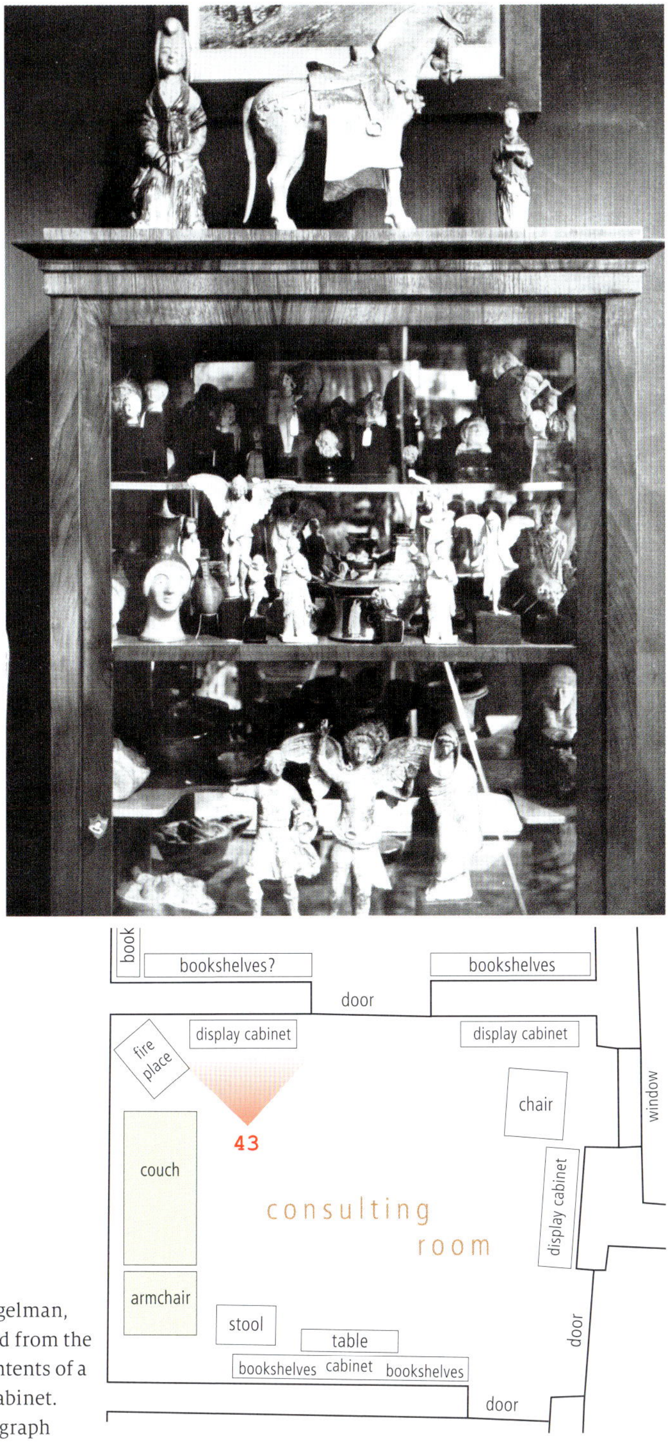

43| Edmund Engelman, View, as obtained from the couch, of the contents of a glazed display cabinet. May 1938. Photograph

of that sort was to be avoided. In that text, based on the methods he had established through his own experience, Freud had, indeed, warned that, in proceeding systematically, one would arrive only at what had already been gleaned from that experience. In order to learn more, it was necessary to proceed intuitively. One ought, indeed, to expose oneself to the impact of all that was seemingly "without cohesion and chaotically disorganised" in order, by that means, to permit the emergence of interconnections as yet unidentified.[96] In this sense, Freud's collection represented a transference of an auditory form of "versatile attentiveness"[97] to objects that could be grasped both visually and haptically. The role of listening in Freud's psychoanalytic practice and the way he positioned the items in his collection here proved mutually supportive.

In a letter of 7th February 1931, to Stefan Zweig, Freud attended to this very interconnection. He objected to his own reputation as a person of "*petit-bourgeois* correctitude" in pointing out that he collected, just as he smoked, in a positively obsessive manner. Zweig should know that "despite my supposed frugality, I have made many sacrifices for my collection of Greek, Roman and Egyptian antiquities, and have really read more of archaeology than of psychology".[98] Freud then went on to speak of "the technique of free association [...] as the most significant innovation in psychoanalysis".[99]

Be it in intimate conversation, in the context of meetings, or in Freud's perpetual dialogue with himself, in addition to the great deal of talking that took place as part of his psychoanalytic practice, communication appears to have been fostered in a context where the presence and arrangement of the collection itself played a part. One of the earliest witnesses to observe this and to leave a record of it was Hanns Sachs. After the day's work was done, they would gather with Freud in his study in order to converse, often remaining there until midnight: "Under the silent stare of idols and animal-shaped gods we listened to some new articles by Freud or read and discussed our own products or just talked about things that interested us".[100] If such an episode was in due course to be characterised as "one

96 Sigmund Freud, "Ratschläge für den Arzt bei der psychoanalytischen Behandlung", in: *SFG*, vol. 12, pp. 367–77, here 370.

97 Sigmund Freud, "Ratschläge für den Arzt bei der psychoanalytischen Behandlung", in: *SFG*, vol. 12, pp, 367–77, here 370.

98 Letter of 7th February 1931 from Sigmund Freud to Stefan Zweig, in: Freud 1968, pp. 420–21.

99 Letter of 7th February 1931 from Sigmund Freud to Stefan Zweig, in: Freud 1968, pp. 420–21. On this technique cf. Tögel 1994, pp. 91–94; Tögel 2013, pp. 84–88; Tögel 2019, p. 65.

100 Sachs 1945, p. 80.

of the key scenes in the history of psychoanalysis",[101] then it is necessary to acknowledge within it the presence of those mute observers.

Ludwig Binswanger, the Swiss psychoanalyst and a long-established close associate of Freud, albeit without ever becoming a true "Freudian", was the first to describe, in connection with his visit to Vienna in late February 1907, how Freud himself engaged with the items in his collection. In this case, the evening's discussion took place "after a day full of work and effort, in [Freud's] silent, penumbral study, which even then contained some important pieces from Classical Antiquity and examples of art from the Middle East and the Far East".[102] And, on this occasion, the items in the collection were by no means of secondary significance:

> "Freud sat at his desk, smoking a cigar, his hands on the arms of the chair or resting in front of him, now and again taking up a figure or an object and looking intently at this interlocutor in a fashion both acute and benevolent, never seeking to demonstrate his own superiority, instructing us not so much theoretically as through instances of a sort of casuistry".[103]

In Binswanger's reference to a "casuistic" way of proceeding there are echoes of that element of psychoanalytic practice whose adherents categorically avoided following a plan. For, they argued, it was only through employing an intellectually playful manner that one might hope to attain those levels of understanding that were inaccessible to rationality on account of its censoring tendency.

Hanns Sachs recounted how Freud would discuss the items in his collection with his closest colleagues and friends in the light of the latest scholarly publications: "Studying with eagerness the descriptions and illustrations, he drew comparisons with his own treasured possessions".[104] Above all, however, Sachs confirmed Binswanger's observation that Freud, while he was himself speaking, would take up an item and seem to communicate with it, both through sight and through touch. This he did not do, however, when he was listening to others speak.[105] Such instances of the connection between linguistic utterance and both haptic comprehension and attentive observation contradict the common assumption that Freud communicated exclusively linguistically. Reflected speech was, for him, interconnected with both tactility and visuality.

101 Phillips 1997, p. 158.
102 Binswanger 1956, p. 11.
103 Binswanger 1956, p. 12.
104 Sachs 1945, p. 99.
105 Sachs 1945, p. 99.

4. The role of images in analytical practice

The supposed exclusivity of the spoken word

The notion that it was solely Freud's analytical practice that necessitated the use, in the consulting room, of his renowned couch is among the chief persisting legends of early psychoanalysis. The armchair occupied by the analyst was positioned just beyond the head-end of the couch and at an angle of 90 degrees to it (Fig. 44),[106] with the result that doctor and patient, despite their physical proximity, could neither touch each other nor maintain eye-contact.

With this supposed fixation on the spoken word, which reduced sensory participation to the ear and to the mouth,[107] Freud distinguished his own analytical

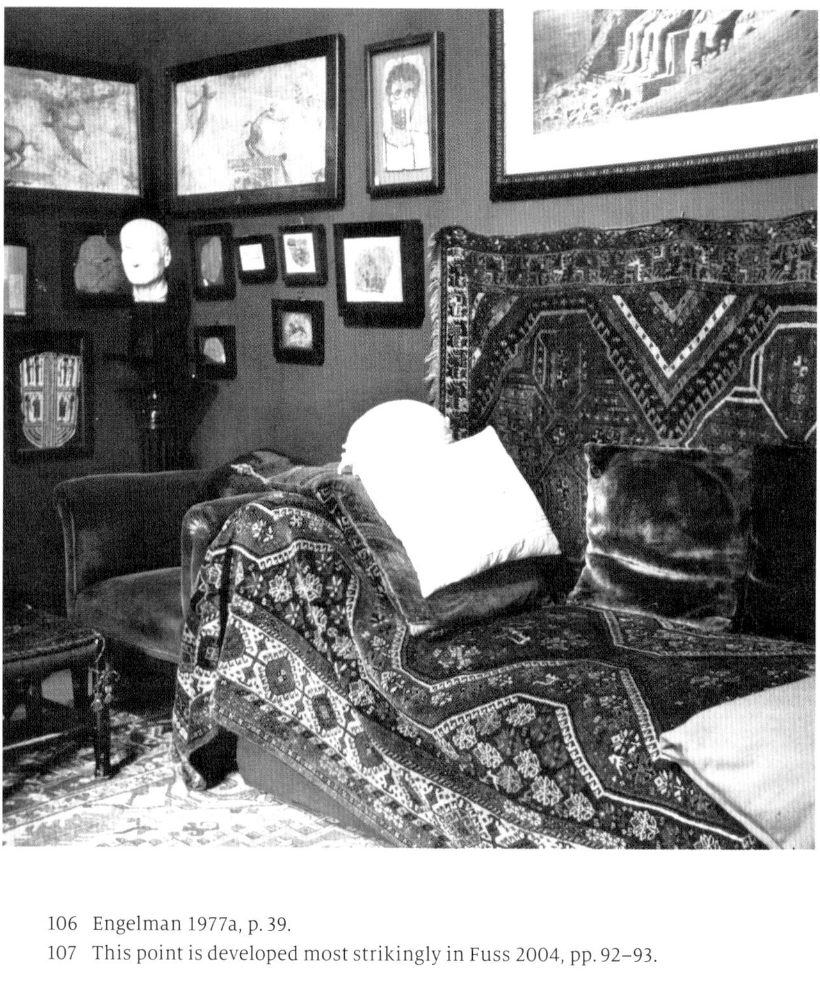

106 Engelman 1977a, p. 39.

107 This point is developed most strikingly in Fuss 2004, pp. 92–93.

method from that of the Parisian neurologist Jean-Martin Charcot, whom he nonetheless continued to revere. While Charcot made a point of incorporating into the analytical process his observations of movement and of every visual aspect of the patient, in the interests of attaining the greatest possible proximity and thereby establishing what has, with some justification, been termed an "image of illness",[108] Freud – or so it seemed – had withdrawn the eye as an instrument of analysis. Largely avoiding eye-contact, he focused on the voice of the patient, and the memories, traumas and obsessions conveyed through its sounds. There has, accordingly, arisen a widely shared assumption that "psychoanalytic reality" for Freud counted for much more than the suggestive quality of a work of art.[109]

This interpretation is, however, at best one-sided. Freud wished to avoid eye-contact not because he placed no trust in visual evidence, but because, for him, eye-contact in the consulting room with one patient after another would have

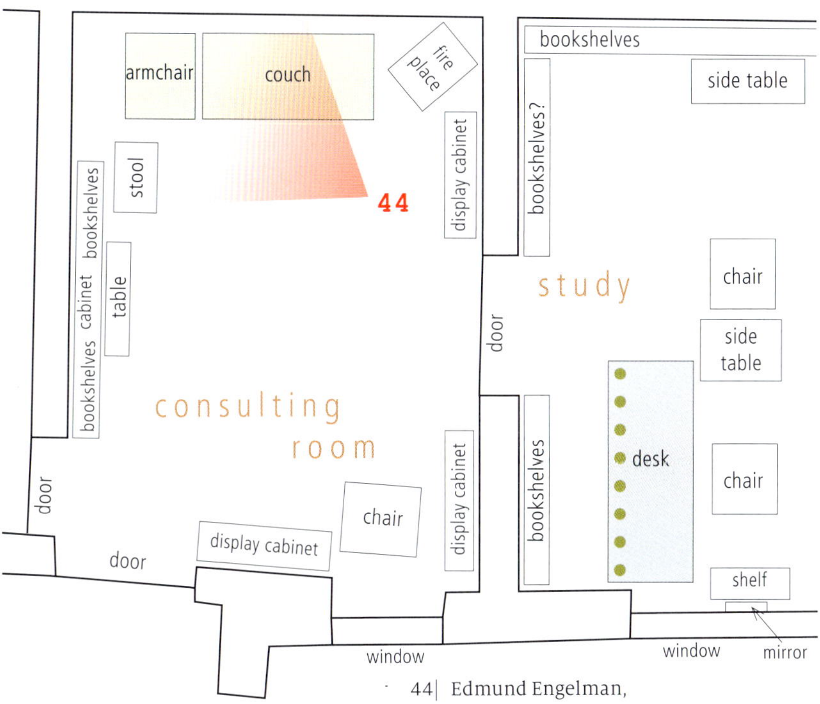

44| Edmund Engelman, Positioning of Freud's armchair beyond the head-end of the couch. May 1938. Photograph

108 Mayer 1998, p. 51.
109 Forrester 1998, p. 28.

been simply unbearable. In 1913, the year in which he worked most intensively on his article on Michelangelo's *Moses*, he justified his own procedure, whereby "one has the patient recline, while one sits behind him", explaining that he could not bear to spend "eight hours a day (or more) being stared at by someone. Because, as I listen to a patient, I may allow myself to become distracted, this does not mean that I wish to offer my own facial expressions as a source of distraction for him or, by this means, to influence what he has to say".[110] However problematic Freud found it to submit his own facial expressions to interpretation, it was also the case that he did not want to give his patient the satisfaction of being able to observe him, because a desire to do so was itself often an aspect of the illness: "The patient often reacts to the situation within which he is constrained as if it were a privation and struggles against it, especially if there is a significant element of voyeurism in his neurosis. And so I insist upon this rule".[111] Elsewhere in the same text Freud explains further: "A great many patients seek to resist being required to recline on the couch while the doctor sits behind them, invisible to them; and they ask to be permitted to undergo the treatment in another position, in most cases because they feel they cannot bear the prospect of not being able to look at the analyst. Such a request is almost always refused".[112] The reason for this was, however, by no means that Freud regarded the visual as insignificant, let alone superfluous. Rather, he recognised that it had an almost medusa-like power. Through his own favoured arrangement for the positioning of both analyst and analysand, he sought to neutralise the personal challenges that inevitably played a part in every session of analysis.

The Rat Man and the Wolf Man

A somewhat less rigid method of avoiding direct eye-contact entailed Freud incorporating items from his collection into the analytical procedure. Doing so enabled him to exploit an intervening realm upon which the eyes of the patient and those of the analyst might both be focused without either of them needing to look at the other. For Freud, the small sculpted figures embodied everything that he had in mind when invoking the analogy between the activity of the archaeologist and the explorations of the unconscious effected by the psychoanalyst. Patient and doctor would be bound through their mutual attention to these archaeological finds, each of them excavated from the earth, which corresponded

110 Sigmund Freud, "Zur Einleitung der Behandllung", in: *SFG*, vol. 13, pp. 119–41, here 131.

111 Sigmund Freud, "Zur Einleitung der Behandlung", in: *SFG*, vol. 13, pp. 119–41, here 131.

112 Sigmund Freud, "Zur Einleitung der Behandlung", in: *SFG*, vol. 13, p. 136.

to those traumas and obsessions buried deepest within the psyche. In the account of his treatment of the Rat Man, Freud spoke of this aspect of his procedure. He had reinforced his statement that the unconscious itself remained relatively constant "through a reference to the antiquities installed in my room". They were in fact "merely items retrieved from a grave; burial in ash signified for them their preservation. It is only now, having been rediscovered, that Pompeii is beginning to perish".[113]

All further statements on this point came from this analysand and from a second, the so-called Wolf Man, who underwent psychoanalysis with Freud between 1910 and 1914. He was, in all probability, the first patient to have recorded the impression that Freud's collection would make on a visitor:

> "I can remember, as if I had seen them earlier today, the two rooms Freud used for his work, linked by an open door, with windows that overlooked a small courtyard in which it was always quiet. The sight alone of these two rooms would have surprised anyone, for they were not at all reminiscent of what one would expect to find in a doctor's surgery, but resembled, rather, the office of an archaeologist. Here, that is to say, one might discover statues of every sort and other quite extraordinary objects, which everyone, even a layman, would immediately recognise as archaeological discoveries deriving from the remote past of Ancient Egypt. Distributed across the walls, too, were stone tablets depicting various scenes from the same epoch".[114]

When questioned by this patient about his great interest in archaeology, Freud had repeated what was, for him, the central analogy between archaeology and psychoanalysis: "Freud himself accounted for his own liking for archaeology in explaining that the psychoanalyst, like the archaeologist engaged in an excavation, was constrained to expose many layers within the psyche of each of his patients before he could access the most valuable of those, which however was also the one that was buried the deepest".[115]

The British psychoanalyst Roger Money-Kyrle reported, ten years after he had himself undergone psychoanalysis (in 1922–25), that Freud had on several occasions interrupted their sessions in the consulting room and invited his patient into the study to show him some fossils: *euhapsis* (of the family *castoridae*), an extinct form of beaver, explaining that "their colour was fading because they had

113 Sigmund Freud, "Bemerkungen über einen Fall von Zwangsneurose", in: *SFG*, vol. 11, pp. 331–401, here 349.

114 Gardiner 1972, p. 174.

115 Gardiner 1972, p. 174.

been dug up – like relics [retrieved] from the unconscious.[116] Yet again it was the interconnection between archaeology (here, more specifically, palaeozoology) and psychoanalysis that Freud saw at play.

Suzanne Cassirer Bernfeld

A further ten years later the aforementioned Suzanne Cassirer Bernfeld (at that point still Suzanne Cassirer Paret) agreed to be analysed by Freud as part of her own training in psychoanalysis. It was during her time with Freud that she learnt what a great significance the sculpted figures in his collection had assumed for him in connection with every aspect of exchange and encounter occurring in his psychoanalytic practice. Of their first meeting – when they were still primarily concerned with getting to know each other and had not yet advanced to discussing the possibility of an analysis – Cassirer Bernfeld reported:

> "And so I went in. And it was all so different to what I had imagined. One has, in any case, to bear in mind that I, at that point, had no idea why I was there. Here, in short, was an immensely nice old man prepared to spend two hours with me in lively conversation – and on every possible subject. I chiefly recall our discussion of Rome. And that he showed me some things, and that he was very relaxed".[117]

When asked if she could recall the reasons for Freud's interest in Rome, she replied: "No, I recall only that he very greatly loved it. His was a real love, as was later to be demonstrated. I had lived in Rome for a long time, and I don't believe I have ever heard a better formulation regarding Rome than that which he had put to [Wilhelm] Fliess: that it [the city of Rome] had been unable to overcome its own desire for Freud".[118]

If Cassirer Bernfeld here transposed, in error, the words "Rome" and "Freud", thereby characterising the Eternal City as a projection of Freud's affection for himself, then this belongs among the slips of the tongue that Freud had analysed in his *Psychopathology of Everyday Life*. Freud is Rome, Rome is Freud. In the understanding of Michelangelo's *Moses* that Freud had eventually attained, an equivalence of this sort actually came about.

Both Rome and Freud's collection were also to play a significant role in the analysis that followed. As Cassirer Bernfeld recalled, "what appeared to me to be

116 Money-Kyrle 1979, p. 267. Cf. Cremerius 1981, p. 134.
117 Cassirer Bernfeld 1953 / 1959 (April 1959, p. 2).
118 Cassirer Bernfeld 1953 / 1959 (April 1959, p. 2).

so remarkable was the fact that, with anyone he agreed to take on as a patient, he conducted himself in the same relaxed and generous manner – we sat in his library [= study] and he showed me all sorts of things and asked me all sorts of questions, though chiefly concerning Rome, how I liked it there, and what I had especially liked, and so on – I mean: it was not as if he didn't have an enormous waiting list [of prospective patients]!"[119] In this case it is clear that the analysis itself became a means of enabling Freud to talk about Rome and to discuss the sculpted figures in his collection with someone with views and tastes similar to his own. The presence of Suzanne Cassirer Bernfeld was, in effect, a pretext for conversation about Rome and about the collection.

An anecdote may here serve to illustrate the relaxation made possible through Freud's ability, in such a context, to engage with his sculpted figures. To one session Cassirer Bernfeld brought an old, poorly preserved Chinese statuette. She was well aware of how angrily Freud could react to any unpunctuality; and, because she was running late and had realised that she would be unable to arrive on time for her appointment, she hoped to be able to use the Chinese figure as a diversion:

> "I asked that he forgive me and told him that I had brought a figure for him. And he took it in his hand, and in the very moment that he looked at it, one could see that he never wanted to let go of it. He had at once fallen in love with the figure, had taken it in his hand, and he said: 'Are you giving me this so as to ensure a reconciliation?' And I said: 'No, nothing of the sort!' Then he said: 'Is it a parting gift?' And I said: 'No, nothing of that sort either!' Then he said: 'So, what do you *want* to do?' And I said: 'I would like to have that [the Chinese figure] analysed'".

Cassirer Bernfeld of course really wanted to be analysed herself; but, in place of herself, she referred to "that", ostensibly meaning the Chinese figure. Through using the figure in this way, she had herself entered into the game, and Freud at once gave her a new appointment. even though he already had a lot of people on his waiting list: "There'll be hell to pay – but damn it! Come to me again on Monday at 9.00".[120]

In her study *Freud and Archeology*, published in 1951, Suzanne Cassirer Bernfeld writes of "the Professor" as himself effectively "on the couch" because it was so clear that he used the statuettes in his collection to overcome traumas of his own. As she was to observe on another occasion, Freud's archaeological objects

119 Cassirer Bernfeld 1953 / 1959 (April 1959, pp. 3–4).
120 Cassirer Bernfeld 1953 / 1959, 7th May 1953, II, pp. 26–27.

were, for him, themselves in part alive. On one hand, as objects that had been buried and then later retrieved, they equated to deceased family members; but, on the other, they could again and again be restored to life through the attention paid to them.[121] An equivalent to this was to be observed in Freud's approach to his sessions with an analysand: "Freud often used his collection to elucidate certain interpretations in his analysis".[122]

Hilda Doolittle

Probably the most impressive witness to the introduction of sculpted figures from Freud's collection into his approach to analysis was the expatriate American writer Hilda Doolittle (Fig. 45). Encouraged and promoted, in London in the 1910s, by her compatriot Ezra Pound, to whose *Imagist* circle she was an early recruit, she left England in 1923 for Switzerland.

In 1933 she went to Vienna in order to undergo psychoanalysis with Sigmund Freud, returning for further sessions the following year.[123] The volume she published in 1956, *Tribute to Freud*, reveals, through its associative style, something of the structure of the collection, in response to which, as she describes most touchingly, she was at first rendered speechless:

> "Automatically, I walk through the door. It closes. Sigmund Freud does not speak. He is waiting for me to say something. I can not speak. I look around the room. A lover of Greek art, I am automatically taking stock of the room's contents. Pricelessly lovely objects are displayed here on the shelves to right, to left of me".[124]

As Doolittle went on to report, it was clear that Freud valued silence, in accordance with rhetorical tradition, as a superior form of speech,[125] and as a token of acknowledgement: "But waiting and finding that I would not or could not speak, he uttered. What he said – and I thought a little sadly – was, 'You are the only person who has ever come into this room and looked at the things in the room before

121 Cassirer Bernfeld 1953 / 1959, p. 119; cf. Bernfeld & Cassirer Bernfeld 1988, p. 250–51.

122 Cassirer Bernfeld 1951, p. 110.

123 Müller 2019, pp. 217–39; here also on what follows, which is limited to Doolittle's accounts of the introduction of the small sculptures.

124 Doolittle 1956, p. 146.

125 Wohlfart & Kreuzer 1992; Bentheim 2006; Mayer 2007. On silence in psychoanalysis: Cremerius 1984, vol. I, pp. 17–54.

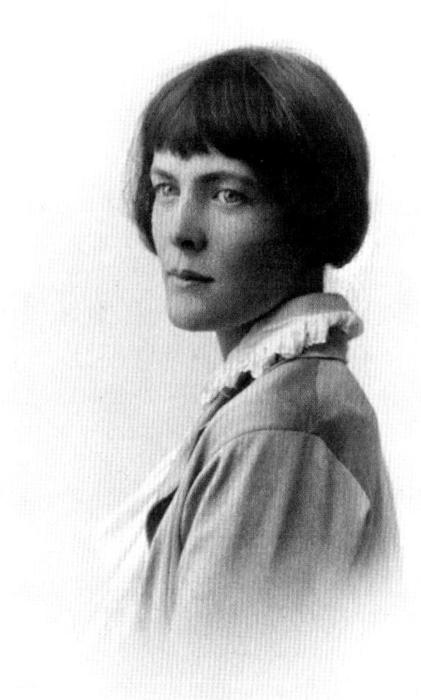

45| Anonymous, Hilda Doolittle, c. 1923. Photograph

looking at me'"[126] Explaining her first reaction, Doolittle told Freud: "[...] no one had told me that this room was lined with treasures. I was to greet the Old Man of the Sea, but no one had told me of the treasures he had salvaged from the sea-depth".[127]

No less interesting than Doolittle's vivid description of the impact upon her of her first encounter with Freud's collection are her hints at how she found within it models for aspects of her own mental life:

> "My imagination wandered at will, my dreams were revealing, and many of them drew on classical or Biblical symbolism. Thoughts were things, to be collected, collated, analysed, shelved or resolved. Fragmentary ideas, apparently unrelated, were often found to be part of a special layer or stratum of thought and memory, therefore to belong together; these were sometimes skilfully pieced together like the exquisite Greek tear-jars and iridescent glass bowls and vases that gleamed in the dusk from the shelves of the cabinet that faced me when I stretched propped up on the couch in the room in Berggasse

126 Doolittle 1956, p. 148.
127 Doolittle 1956, p. 147.

> 19, Wien IX. The dead were living in so far as they lived in memory or were recalled in dream."[128]

The possibility, "gleaming" among the items on display, of bringing together a variety of unconnected fragments of memory has a distinctly surreal quality, which was to ensure it would appeal to the artistic avant-garde.

It was not the case that Freud always sat, invisible to the analysand, beyond the head-end of the couch. He would sometimes move about the consulting room, or walk between it and the study, in order to make the dialogue between himself and the patient into a trialogue that also accommodated the sculpted figures: "He had taken up one of the figures on the desk. He was holding it in his hand and looking at me. This, I surmised, was the image that he thought would interest me the most".[129]

Doolittle responded to this interplay with questions of her own:

> "I did not always know if the Professor's excursions with me into the other room were by way of distraction, actual social occasions, or part of his plan. Did he want to find out how I would react to certain ideas embodied in these little statues, or how deeply I felt the dynamic *idea* still implicit in spite of the fact that ages and aeons of time had flown over many of them? Or did he mean simply to imply that he wanted to share his treasures with me, those tangible shapes before us that yet suggested the intangible and vastly more fascinating treasures of his own mind?"[130]

Yet Doolittle nonetheless repudiated this sceptical view of the situation:

> "If it was a *game*, a sort of roundabout way of finding out something that perhaps my unconscious guard or censor was anxious to keep from him, well, I would do my best to play this game, this guessing game – or whatever it was."[131]

It is possible that, when Doolittle alluded in this way to the playfulness of Freud's approach to psychoanalysis, she had in mind Johan Huizinga's immortal text on the *Homo ludens*, which was first published in 1938.[132] It is also possible that she was recalling two well-known passages from the Bible, in both of which the exceptional role of play is emphasised. The first of these concerns praise of the

128 Doolittle 1956, p. 18.
129 Doolittle 1956, p. 101.
130 Doolittle 1956, p. 102.
131 Doolittle, 1956, p. 103.
132 Huizinga 1938.

self, as an articulation of the divine wisdom in God's Creation: "Then I was by him, as one brought up with him: and I was daily his delight, rejoicing always before him. / Rejoicing in the habitable part of his earth; and my delights were with the sons of men" (*Proverbs*: 8, 30–31).[133] The equating of creation and play relates to the traditional belief that the God of the Creation had proceeded playfully in forming the cosmos, concerned above all to ensure that no element in the created world stood above Him. Doolittle may have understood Freud's collection as itself a sort of creation informed by the spirit of play, in which she, too, became a player such as that described in the biblical text.

In the second, no less celebrated biblical passage, God introduces Job (who has been contesting His will) to Leviathan and to Behemoth, monsters respectively of the sea and of the land, in order then to confront him with the ironic question: "Wilt thou play with him [here = Behemoth] as with a bird?" (*Job*: 41, 5). While, in the *Song of Solomon*, divine wisdom identifies play as the highest form of creative activity, in the *Book of Job* God specifies that inability to play is a proof of weakness. In short: he who is capable of playing is sovereign. Doolittle's own readiness to play along with Freud's approach to analysis points to this interconnection. In a playful fashion, an erotic component may also have been either expressed or restrained here. Freud had, after all, observed: "Every collector is a substitute Don Juan, just as the objects amassed equate to erotica".[134]

During her time in Vienna Doolittle is likely to have come across a painting in the Kunsthistorisches Museum that was especially eloquent on the subject of an individual's strong attachment to his own collection: Titian's portrait of the art dealer and collector Jacopo Strada (Fig. 46).[135] With the four circlets of his gold chain and the medallion affixed to one of them, his costume of velvet and silk, his fur coat and his dagger, Strada is here characterised as a person of some eminence who has, one may imagine, just placed on the table beside him a small marble torso, some coins and a letter addressed to Titian. There is considerable psychological interest in the way Strada is shown in the act of offering a statuette of Venus to a potential buyer. With an air of scrutinising the latter, he holds the figure as if he would rather not sell it and could keep it for himself. Through simultaneous, yet contradictory, gestures of presentation and removal, Titian has here achieved a masterpiece in the treatment of the psychology of possession as this may apply to a work of art.

All this may well have prompted Doolittle to think of Freud and the 1914 etching of him seated at his desk (see Fig. 33) behind a row of small, sculpted figures.

133 On this point, cf. Kehl 1974.

134 Freud 1950, p. 121. I am indebted to Jäger 2023 for this information.

135 Müller 2019, pp. 223–24. On the painting: Fehrenbach 2021, pp. 243–48.

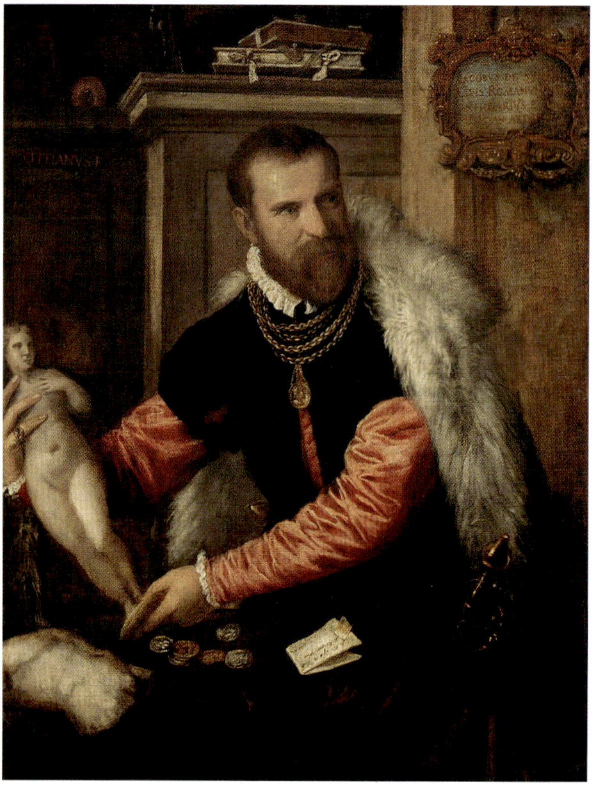

46| Titian, *Portrait of Jacopo Strada*, 1567–68. Oil on canvas. Vienna, Kunsthistorisches Museum

Through the presence of these last Freud's own study was drawn into the history of the *studiolo*, that type of interior in which the scholars of the Renaissance used to display their own collections, as Freud had himself done, albeit in a much more expansive style.[136]

Freud was particularly drawn to a Greek bronze figure of Athena (Fig. 47).[137] This was to be separately smuggled out of Austria by Princess Marie Bonaparte when Freud left Vienna for London in the early summer of 1938, lest the National Socialist authorities, having permitted Freud's collection to follow him, should nonetheless resolve to seize items from it.[138] For Freud, this figure was the incarnation of a Jewish life enabled fully to assimilate into a Christian ambience, with-

136 Liebenwein 1977.

137 *Freud as Collector* 1996, cat. 64, p. 56.

138 Davies 1998, p. 100. Cf. *"Meine... alten und dreckigen Götter"* 1998, cat. 80, pp. 144–45; *Freud's Sculpture* 2006, p. 42.

out thereby committing any betrayal of itself, through a profound, studious immersion in the culture of Ancient Greece. And, in this respect, the figure of Athena was also an embodied symbol of the fact that Freudian psychoanalysis itself made much use of the narrative patterns to be found in Greek mythology, as in the case of the story of Oedipus.[139] Doolittle, in her own memory of Freud, held tightly to this most sensitive context for the development of his psychoanalytic methods:

> "It was a smallish object, judging by the place left empty, my end of the semicircle, made by the symmetrical arrangement of the Gods (or the Goods) on his table. '*This* is my favourite', he said. He held the object toward me. I took it in my hand. It was a little bronze statue, helmeted, clothed to the foot in carved robe with the upper incised chiton or peplum. One hand was extended as if holding a staff or rod: 'She is perfect', he said, '*only she has lost her spear.*' I did not say anything. He knew that I loved Greece. He knew that I loved Hellas. I stood looking at Pallas Athene [...]".[140]

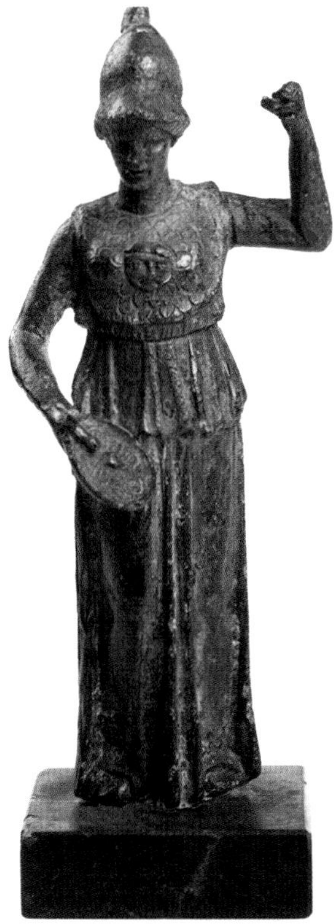

47| Figure of Athena, second century. Bronze. London, Freud Museum, no. 3007

With Doolittle's silence, the sculpted figure again became all the more eloquent a counterpart for Freud. It was a medium through which he could hold fast to his fleeting ideas, even guard against their disappearance.

Sigmund Freud and Arthur Schnitzler as collectors

It was by no means unusual, in Vienna in the years around 1900, that Freud should embark upon assembling a collection of his own. What made his collection unique was no less its character than its arrangement and its setting. Its particularity in all these respects becomes apparent if it compared with the collection assembled

139 On this matter, see the moving, magisterial essay by Carl Schorske 1998.
140 Doolittle 1956, pp. 103–04.

by the Viennese dramatist and novelist Arthur Schnitzler, which had been assembled over approximately the same period. Such a comparison is also of value in that the collectors in question recognised a certain personal affinity. On 4th May 1922, in the letter Freud sent to Schnitzler to mark the latter's sixtieth birthday, he accounted for the fact that he had for so long eschewed establishing direct contact by invoking his own fear of thereby coming face to face with his own *doppelgänger.*[141] Just over a month later, however, on 16th June, Freud invited Schnitzler to call on him at 19 Berggasse, taking the opportunity to introduce this guest to his collection. Schnitzler thereafter noted in his diary: "He was most warmly welcoming [...] Then he showed me his library – his own writings, the many translations of them, the publications of his students – and all manner of antique bronze figurines".[142]

It must have been at once apparent to Schnitzler how greatly Freud's collection differed from his own. In his critique of the ossification of contemporary European culture Schnitzler, as a committed modernist, had initially sought to liberate himself from the legacy of Classical Antiquity, only then to be persuaded by the vitalist re-evaluation in the work of Friedrich Nietzsche to reconsider his own stance, a shift in due course reflected in Schnitzler's approach to collecting.[143] In 1902, when Anton Paul Huber, since 1898 photographer to the Austrian Imperial Court, recorded Schnitzler standing at the high desk in his study, the writer appears as if he were a sounding board for the objects surrounding him (Fig. 48).[144]

Busts of Goethe and Schiller here appear as complementary guardian spirits, the former visible below Schnitzler's right hand, the latter placed on top of a cabinet to the upper right. But all the other items visible in this shot are works from Antiquity, some of them original pieces, others modern reproductions.[145] At Schnitzler's back is a reduced cast of the celebrated *Venus de Milo*, its head and shoulders to be found again in the photograph on the wall directly in front of him. To his right is a copy of a figure excavated in Pompeii and at first taken for a *Narcissus*, though later identified as *Dionysus*. To Schnitzler's right is a photograph of the bust of the so-called *Dying Alexander*, yet another well-established source of the inspiration to be found in the art of Classical Antiquity. Placed next to this image is a miniature copy of the work long known as the *Borghese Gladiator*, while at the extreme upper right is a further photograph: a characteristically androgynous bust of *Antinous*.[146]

141 Freud 1968, p. 357. Cf. Karsten 2018, pp. 28–29, 153–54.

142 Entry for Friday 16th June 1922, here cited from the online edition: schnitzler-tagebuch.aedho.oeaw.ac.at

143 Aurnhammer & von den Hoff 2021, pp. 155–56, 160–64.

144 Aurnhammer & von den Hoff 2021, p. 160, fig. 2b.

145 On this and on what follows: Aurnhammer & von den Hoff 2021, p. 167.

146 Aurnhammer & von den Hoff 2021, pp. 167–74.

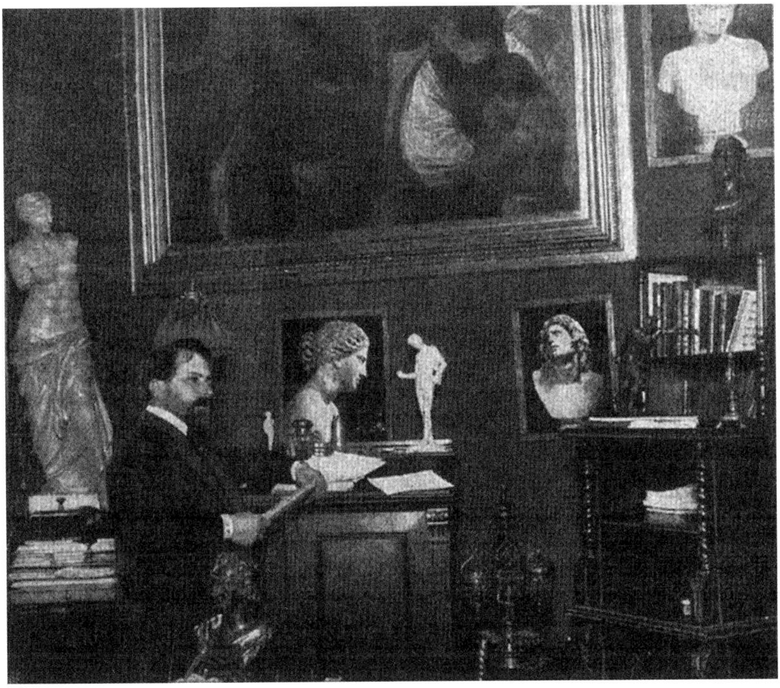

48| Anton Paul Huber, Arthur Schnitzler at home in Vienna. 1902. Photograph

Considered alongside Max Pollak's etching of Freud seated at the desk in his own study (Fig. 33), Huber's photograph of Schnitzler makes clear not only how different were their respective collections but also how distinct was the relationship between each man and the objects he had assembled. Freud, as observed earlier, appears as if ready to engage in a silent dialogue with each of the small, silhouetted figures aligned in front of him. Very compellingly conveyed is a sense of the reciprocal longing for communication achieved through touch. It is as if the idols are waiting for Freud to reach out and take hold of one of them, as if thereby to absorb knowledge of a sort accessible by no other means. While Schnitzler's connection with the works surrounding him is maintained through a web of invisible threads, in the case of Freud it evinces the markedly haptic quality that continued to mean so much to him.

The collection and the life

On 8th October 1938, four months after his arrival in London, Freud wrote to a former patient, Jeanne Lampl-de Groot, about the state of the collection in his and its new home at 20 Maresfield Gardens in Hampstead: "All the Egyptians, the

Chinese and the Greeks have arrived, having suffered very little damage during the journey, and they here look even more imposing than they did in Berggasse. But there's just one thing: a collection to which nothing new is being added is really dead".[147] The "Greeks" to which Freud here referred doubtless included the *Athena*. In what Freud termed the "death" of the collection, this figure, too, will have seemed to him to have lost its "own" life and its significance as a member of an ensemble that, for so long, had grown steadily larger and more animated. This had been the outcome not only of Freud's acquisitions, but also of the items that came to the collection as gifts – as was the case, for example, with a ring made from an antique gem, which Freud had received from Sándor Ferenczi as a token of fidelity.[148] In this respect, it could be said that each of the items also had the character of a talisman attesting to a particular connection with a person or a set of circumstances.

When Ludwig Binswanger visited Freud's widow in 1946, he was overcome by a "most peculiar sensation" when he was "led into a room in which there appeared before my eyes a great many of those works of art that I had already encountered in his study, during my first and subsequent visits to Vienna".[149] It was inevitable that Binswanger should associate these items so closely with Freud that, in Freud's absence, they seemed like ghosts:

> "While I had no difficulty in seeing and responding to the Frau Professor of those days and that of now as one and the same person, the 'dead objects' had something ghostly about them, as if they were indeed revenants. Was it not possible for me to unite their past, which was inseparable from the existence of their former owner, and their present, which without him was imbued with something shadowy and ghostly?"[150]

Hilda Doolittle had conveyed much the same sentiment in her own words: "He is part and parcel of these treasures".[151] Freud was his collection, and his collection, without him, was dead. It was his alter ago.

147 Letter of 8th October 1938 from Sigmund Freud to Jeanne Lampl-de Groot, in: Forrester 1998, pp. 21–22.

148 Marinelli 1998, p. 10; Forrester 1998, p. 24.

149 Binswanger 1956, p. 120.

150 Binswanger 1956, p. 120.

151 Doolittle 1956, p. 147.

III THE SECRET WORK OF IMAGES

1. Reasons for the "veiling" of images

Freud's preoccupation with Michelangelo's *Moses* was shaped by the powerful effect that this sculpted figure had had on the way he felt able to define himself and his own scientific theories. The intensity of Freud's obsession with the figure was owed to the fact that he associated the self-mastery he found so dynamically embodied there with his own conflict with C. G. Jung, and thus with the obligation he at length recognised not to react in the merciless manner of the Moses of *Exodus* to the apostasy of the Israelites. Freud was, however, aware that he would not have been able to rise to an equivalent of that. As mentioned earlier, his hesitation in publishing his analysis of Michelangelo's figure is explained by the extent of his own emotional involvement in what, for this reason, he felt to be a "non-analytical interpretation".

All those who found themselves in Freud's consulting room at 19 Berggasse would have immediately recognised the particular significance that his assembled idols had for him. And this was, above all, the case when Freud was moved to present an item from the collection to one of his patients, as had been the case with the Munich philosopher Willy Haas. On occasion, some of Freud's patients, among them Josefa Ehrenhöfer, would present him with an antique figurine to add to the collection. And Freud's emerging friendship with Marie Bonaparte was to be marked by repeated instances of the exchange of gifts.[1] Beyond this circle of patients and friends there appears, however, to have been no mention of the collection. As Hilda Doolittle was to observe: "I [had] been told about the Professor, his family, his way of life. I [had] heard certain personal memories not available to the general readers of his books. I [had] heard him lovingly criticized by his admirers and soundly berated by his enemies".[2] She had, accordingly, expected to

1 *SFG*, vol. 22 / 1, p. 500 (Haas), p. 398 (Ehrenhöfer); *SFG*, vol. 22 / 2, p. 874 (gift from Freud's to Bonaparte), p. 954 (gift from Bonaparte to Freud).

2 Doolittle 1956, p. 148.

meet a scholar and a physician who had, in every respect, mastered, in a purely metaphorical sense, the idea of the vast ocean of all that was unknowable. But, as she would go on to say, "no one had told me that this room was lined with treasures. I was to greet the Old Man of the Sea, but no one had told me of the treasures he had salvaged from the sea-depth. He is at home here. He is part and parcel of these treasures".[3] And yet, for all the importance of Freud's collection, both for himself and in the context of the psychoanalytic procedures that he had evolved, there is no reference to it in his published writings, with the exception of his short report on the case of the Rat Man.[4]

It is likely that an explanation lies in the obsessive nature of Freud's identification with his collection, a characteristic in marked contrast to the objective distance he would have been urged to observe at every stage of his own training and would in turn have recommended to his own students. He had, after all, compared his own passion for collecting with his addiction to smoking.[5]

Here, too, Freud's relationship with C. G. Jung must have played a part. The nominal line separating Freud from Jung and from the latter's own circle could, as Freud envisaged it, hardly have been clearer and sharper; and one inevitable result of this was that Freud felt ever less inclined to acknowledge Jung's own, systematic incorporation of images into his own understanding of the history of psychoanalysis. If Freud had recognised that his own close identification with the items in his collection was itself of relevance to analysis, it would soon have become apparent that, in this matter, there was really more that united Freud and Jung than separated them.[6] Jung would, to some degree, have been rehabilitated; and it is possible that it was for this reason that Freud continued not to comment in print on the strong connection he felt with the items in his own collection.[7]

It is possible that a further reason for Freud's preference for "veiling" the visual and haptic dimension of his psychoanalytic practice lay in the international dispute that had arisen over Jean-Martin Charcot's approach to psychiatry, with its dependence on images and apparatus. Freud had himself been able to observe this at first hand in Paris in the mid-1880s. The Parisian neurologist was accused of having employed apparatus during his experiments in hypnosis which made it more likely that the hoped-for outcome would indeed occur. One of those to emerge as a fierce critic of Charcot in this respect was Hippolyte Bernheim, who

3 Doolittle 1956, p. 147.

4 Sigmund Freud, "Bemerkungen über einen Fall von Zwangsneurose", in: *SFG*, vol. 11, pp. 331–401, here 349.

5 Letter of 7th February 1931 from Sigmund Freud to Stefan Zweig, in Freud 1968, pp. 420–21. See above pp. 74.

6 Kuspit 1989, p. 145.

7 On Freud as the "great veiler" ("*grosser Verhüller*"): Cremerius 1971.

taught at Nancy. Bernheim argued that the instruments used by Charcot and his colleagues seemed to function so well only because both doctors and patients had been virtually inculcated with a belief in their efficacy. Bernheim called for a "dematerialisation" of analysis.[8] Freud was especially familiar with the objections raised by Bernheim, not least because he had translated the latter's volume of 1887, *De la suggestion et de son application à la thérapeutique*.[9] In 1889, moreover, Freud visited Bernheim in Nancy.

Freud was no less aware that German psychiatrists themselves continued to insist that investigation into hypnosis eschew any resort to images and apparatus.[10] It is possible that Freud overtly complied with this expectation in order not himself to be counted, as were the Parisians, among the "fetishists".[11] In concealing the visual aspect of his own psychoanalytic practice, Freud ironically fulfilled his own theory of fetishism in so far as this entailed acting in a performative fashion while yet resorting to both masking and "veiling".[12]

2. Overcoming the prohibition of images

Vasari's account

While some or all of these factors may have played a part in inducing Freud to "veil" his image-related activities, they cannot have proved decisive because their tactical nature was of the sort to which he would never yield when the essence of a method was at stake. The question as to a theological justification was of a different kind. For Freud, the image-related issue of which every Jewish individual, whether or not a believer, would have been aware had to be taken into account. The Second Commandment unambiguously declared: "Thou shalt have no other gods before me. / Thou shalt not make unto thee any graven image, or any likeness of any thing that is in heaven above, or that is in the earth beneath, or that is in the water under the earth. / Thou shalt not bow down thyself to them, nor serve them" (*Exodus*: 20, 3–5).

This prohibition related to three-dimensional images, in effect to idols. Freud, had he read Giorgio Vasari's life of Michelangelo, would have been particularly struck by what that author had observed of the *Moses*: "And the Jews, both men and women, may well continue to come in great numbers every Saturday, as they do now, to see it and revere it: not as something human, but as something

8 Mayer 2001, pp. 176–78; Mayer 2002, pp. 65–88; cf. Jäger 2023.
9 Bernheim 1888. On this complex, cf. also Armstrong 2021.
10 Cf. Tögel 2006, p. 22; and Mayer 2001, pp. 192–93.
11 Mayer 2001, pp. 177–78.
12 Böhme 2006, p. 408.

divine (*non cosa umana, ma divina*)".[13] There is, however, no secure evidence that Freud had read Vasari's text.[14] But in the seventh (1912) edition of the guide book by Theodor Gsell Fels, *Rom und die Campagna*, to which he certainly had referred, Vasari's statement was paraphrased. And Freud had noted, with a marginal mark, the following passage: "This Moses, which Michelangelo had invested with his own deep feeling, and to which he had given his own Promethean power, so overwhelmingly embodies the highest visual conception of the Old Testament lawgiver, priest and prophet that large parties of Roman Jews came to visit it every Saturday in order to hail their 'Capitano'".[15]

And so, at least by means of this secondary source, Freud would have been familiar with Vasari's claim that the Jews of Rome felt sufficiently drawn to Michelangelo's *Moses* as to engage in what might even be described as a form of pilgrimage. Vasari had here, moreover, touched on a crucial point. The *Moses* was shown holding those Tablets of the Law upon which the prohibition of images was inscribed. For any Jew who was prepared to adhere to that prohibition, Michelangelo's figure was a self-contradiction preserved in marble.[16]

The prohibition of images as a component of the faith of the Jews

For Freud, this conflict must have been of considerable interest. In his intention to replace religious faith with science, he was militantly anti-religious; but his identity as a member of the Jewish community was, for him, non-negotiable. After his move to London he told Israel Cohen, General Secretary of the World Zionist Organization, of his determination not in any way to be viewed or treated as a figurehead on account of his atheism: he was sure "that my absolutely negative position towards every religion, including Judaism, distinguishes me from the majority of our fellow Jews".[17] He did, however, introduce this assertion with the no less apodictic confession, that he was "a good Jew, who never denied Judaism".[18] This conflict characterised Freud's relationship with images.

As Freud was to argue in *Moses and Monotheism*, the prohibition of images was, for him, an important element within the Jewish community: "Among the

13 Vasari 1568 III, p. 727. Cf. Blum 2008, pp. 80–82.

14 While the evidence offered in Mary Bergstein 2010, pp. 53, 55 is very plausible, it cannot be verified.

15 Gsell Fels 1912, cols. 752–53.

16 Blum 2008, pp. 83–85.

17 Letter from Sigmund Freud to Israel Cohen, here cited after Tögel 2019, p. 103. Freud had condensed the same statement in 1928 into three words: he was, he claimed, "an infidel Jew" ("*ein ungläubiger Jude*") (Sigmund Freud, "Ein religiöses Erlebnis", in: *SFG*, vol. 19, pp. 15–20, here 18).

18 Here cited after Tögel 2019, p. 103.

principles of the Mosaic religion, there is one that is of more significance than may at first be recognised. It is a prohibition on the making of images, that is to say the demand that one worship a god that one cannot see".[19] Presumably arising in recognition of the need for precautionary measures against the "magical abuse" of images, their prohibition must have "had a far-reaching effect. For it signified a repudiation of sensory perception in favour of an idea that has to be termed abstract: a triumph of the spiritual over the sensorial and, strictly speaking, a renunciation of instinctive drives, which would itself incur a certain psychological outcome".[20]

This explanation of the prohibition of images, which in its character could be acknowledged as a process of spiritualisation, has led to the assumption that Freud persisted in developing his own form of psychoanalysis as a means of redeeming, even of surpassing, the Jewish prohibition of images.[21] Freudian psychoanalysis could, in that sense, be seen to stand in the same tradition, with its iconoclastic limitation to sound, specifically that of the words exchanged between doctor and patient. As a means towards a greater spiritualisation, Freudian psychoanalysis could, indeed, also appear to be a model of the intellectual consolidation of a new science, such as was then to be observed in research into hysteria and in other fields of scientific enquiry.[22]

In view of the central importance that questions of visuality were already assuming in other areas of scholarship, this interpretation initially seems plausible. In Arnold Schönberg's innovations in the treatment of harmony, which were to be applied explicitly in his work of 1930–32 on Acts I and II of his unfinished opera *Moses and Aaron*, the renunciation of what was aurally appealing in a conventional sense seemed to be a form of musical iconoclasm, reacting to the Mosaic prohibition of images.[23] With the destruction of the Mosaic Tablets of the Law, Schönberg radicalised the biblical prohibition, leaving his work in a fragmentary form, and so ultimately giving silence the last word.[24] The iconoclastic "triumph of spirituality", of which Freud was later to write in *Moses and Monotheism*, accorded with this earlier stage in his reflections on this matter.

19 Sigmund Freud, "Der Mann Moses und die monotheistische Religion", in: *SFG*, vol. 20, pp. 223–347, here 325.

20 Sigmund Freud, "Der Mann Moses und die monotheistische Religion", in: *SFG*, vol. 20, pp. 223–347, here 325.

21 Assmann 2002, pp. 162–69. Jan Assmann envisaged this attempt as a revision of the chapter on Freud's book on Moses in his great work on Moses the Egyptian: *Moses der Ägypter* (Assmann 1998), which in itself already demands respect as a triumph of scholarly courage. The present text is a plea for a revision of that revision.

22 Bredekamp 2005.

23 Schäfer 2002; here cited after Schäfer 2003, pp. 32–36; Germer 2011, pp. 337–44.

24 Germer 2011, p. 344.

The compulsory character of the prohibition of images

It is thus all the more necessary to emphasise that Freud in fact used this apparent approval for a heightened spirituality as an occasion to point to its destructive consequences. In *Civilization and its Discontents*, he would see the increasing "sense of guilt" that accompanied every cultural advance as the source of neuroses and an insatiable instinct for destruction.[25] The spiritualising "super-ego", his text continues, "cares too little, in the rigour of its commandments and prohibitions, about the happiness of the ego".[26] The same was true of the "cultural-super-ego". This "issues a commandment without first ascertaining if it is possible for humanity to observe it".[27] And, because it could not, and thus did not, the denial of the instincts compelled in this fashion would bring forth feelings of fear and guilt.[28]

It was for this reason that Freud opposed to a positive appraisal of the prohibition of images an insistence on the need to resist its negative consequences. Freud's identification with Michelangelo's *Moses*, his no less strong sense of a connection with his own collection, and his concern to incorporate items from this into his psychoanalytic practice all stood in effective opposition to the "cultural-super-ego" and the prohibition of images, and thereby countered the perception of psychoanalysis as itself iconoclastic. What this demonstrated was, rather, a variant on Freud's "*triumph* over the Jewish religion".[29] But this would not issue in what Freud called a "triumph of spirituality", but in a struggle against its constraints and against the fear that these incurred.

25 On the Fall of Man, by way of the violence of thought, patricide and the totemistic role of the father, to Christ's assumption of guilt: Ernst 2015.

26 Sigmund Freud, "Das Unbehagen in der Kultur", in: *SFG*, vol. 19, pp. 61–134, here 132.

27 Sigmund Freud. "Das Unbehagen in der Kultur", in: *SFG*, vol. 19, pp. 61–134, here 132.

28 Schäfer 2003, pp. 22–23.

29 Schäfer 2003, pp. 24–25.

3. Images as a condition of freedom

Unatonable guilt

The nature of the punishment that Moses was prepared to impose upon his people reveals what was here at stake. To begin with, he had the Golden Calf melted down, then crushed until it was of the consistency of flour that could be scattered on the waters, which the Israelites were then ordered to drink. (*Exodus*: 32, 20).[30] A further punishment, however, is seldom mentioned, on account of its cruelty. It consisted in Moses commanding the Levites, who had gathered around him in the name of God, to "put every man his sword by his side, and go in and out from gate to gate throughout the camp, and slay every man his brother, and every man his companion, and every man his neighbour" (*Exodus*: 32, 27). This command was indeed carried out: "The children of Levi did according to the word of Moses: and there fell of the people that day about three thousand men" (*Exodus*: 32, 28). Hope that this punitive action (punitive also for the murderers) would be followed by a form of reconciliation with God was to be disappointed. While God's punishment would not follow immediately, He pronounced that this would surely follow on an indeterminate Day of Reckoning: "on the day when I visit I will visit their sin upon them" (*Exodus*: 32, 34).

Freud saw in this episode the second reason for the Jews' collective sense of guilt. The first had been that the Israelites – as Freud (to the dismay of many of his readers) was to argue in *Moses and Monotheism* –[31] had murdered their founding father, Moses. On this account they were thereafter constrained to live beneath the oppressive weight of a colossal sense of guilt. It was, however, the second episode that, in due course, issued in the prohibition of images. The Israelites had initially sinned in worshipping the Golden Calf. When they committed the collective murder of their brothers, companions and neighbours, the original guilt had been compounded. But, in spite of those sinful actions, God nonetheless reserved his punishment for a Day of Reckoning. As a result of this, however, the Jewish community continued to live without even the prospect of a future time in which they might at least be relieved of their sense of guilt.

Freud had himself both understood and felt this consequence when he identified with the "rabble" that had drawn the angry gaze of Michelangelo's *Moses*. As he explained, in the introduction to his article on Michelangelo's figure, he had

30 The most comprehensive analysis of the apostasy and its punishment is provided by Sibylle Moser-Ernst and Ursula Marinelli (Moser-Ernst & Marinelli 2011).

31 "It is to be regretted that the Gangsters did not put you into a concentration camp, that's where you belong" (here cited after: *SFG*, vol. 20, p. 224).

always sought "to resist the contemptuous angry stare of the hero"; but he did not always feel able to do so, "and sometimes I have then crept out of the half-darkness of the interior as if I myself belonged among that rabble upon which his eye was fixed."[32] In reacting thus, Freud was himself effectively taking on the collective Jewish consciousness of guilt.

The triumph over guilt

It is against this background that Freud's obsession with surrounding himself with small idols assumes its liberating quality. If, in Freud's consulting room, as in his study, an overpowering abundance of images defined the character of the space, then this all at once declared: the prohibition of images does not hold. In this forest of idols, the guilt complex residing in the unconscious, and there preserving a memory of the dance around the Golden Calf and of the massacre that followed, lost its validity. Archaeology and the antiquities it brought to light were here indisputably in the ascendent: any sense of guilt was opposed by the sheer omnipresence of that which had once been prohibited.[33]

The images defined the consulting room as a symbolic place of liberation, for one was here relieved of any fear – be it regarding the coercive means employed by a religious "super-ego" or the social norms that might compromise obedience to the prevailing commitment to honesty. It was for this reason that items from Freud's collection were to be found only in that space and in the adjoining study, and not elsewhere in the apartment at 19 Berggasse. Together, both of these spaces constituted a sphere of freedom that itself embodied absolute honesty: here there was no authority, no prohibition of images, no fear – and this, as attested by the very diverse geo-cultural origins of the figures, as a universal principle.[34]

Jofi and the idols

The liberation that might be attained through the shock of coming upon an interior full to bursting with idols had, from 1930, a second component in the form of a dog, which almost never left Freud's side. As recalled by his son Martin, the dog was even present during the sessions of analysis: "Then she would lie motionless alongside his desk with the Greek and Egyptian statuettes, while he

32 Sigmund Freud, "Der Moses des Michelangelo", in: SFG, vol. 14, p. 23. Cf. Yerushalmi 1991a, p.76.

33 Cassirer Bernfeld 1951, p. 119; Bernfeld & Cassirer Bernfeld 1988, p. 250.

34 Gallo 2011.

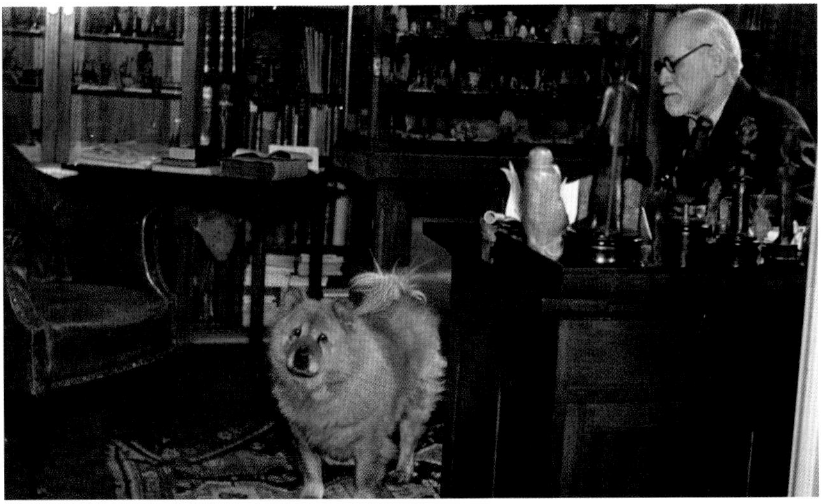

49| Marie Bonaparte, Freud at his desk with his dog, Jofi. 1936. London, Freud Museum. Photograph

concentrated on his treatment of the patients".[35] Moreover, at the very moment the time allotted for a session was up, the dog would yawn.[36]

A new patient might have been prepared to expect almost anything – but not that a dog would be present throughout a session of analysis, even assuming there the role of a sort of custodian. Through its very presence, the dog induced the same sort of astonishment (albeit for different reasons) as did the presence of the collection, the outcome in both cases being an awareness of the space of the consulting room and the study as a zone of liberation.

While a parallel between the pseudo-living sculpted figures and the dog may even seem absurd, compelling visual evidence for it is to be found in one of the most telling photographic portraits of Freud (Fig. 49). This shows him seated at his desk; before him is aligned the palisade of "old and filthy gods" and behind him a stretch of wall features two particularly striking mummy portraits.[37] To the left of the desk is Freud's beloved chow, Jofi, which he had received as a gift, on 9th March 1930, from Princess Marie Bonaparte.[38] This photograph captures

35 Martin Freud 1999, p. 203.

36 Martin Freud 1999, pp. 203–04.

37 On the upper mask: *Sigmund Freud and Art* 1989, p. 73.

38 Letter of 5th March 1930 from Princess Marie Bonaparte to Sigmund Freud, in: Bonaparte / Freud 2022, p. 510; letter of 10th March 1930 from Sigmund Freud to Princess Marie Bonaparte, in: Bonaparte / Freud 2022, p. 511. On Jofi: Jones 1957, pp. 225–27; Clark 1980, pp. 483–84.

extremely well how self-assuredly the dog occupies the space between Freud and his sculpted figures, and how alert she is to the presence of others.

Jofi was the seismograph that guided Freud's first appraisal of individuals as yet unfamiliar to him, who were to be judged through their reaction to this animal. As Suzanne Cassirer Bernfeld notes in the record of her own analysis with Freud: "And then Jofi stood there, and then I gave Jofi a kiss, and now and again Jofi lay down calmly on the floor, and then the Professor said: 'This will be a good hour'. And sometimes Jofi simply left the room".[39] Sometimes, however, she leapt up on to the couch,

> "and did something completely crazy. She stretched out and laid her head on the cushion [...] And I moved over until I was right up against the wall, and Jofi lay there, and that's how we spent the session. And when the hour was up, the Professor said: 'Well, whatever next!' Then he went on: 'Jofi is full of surprises, never before has she done anything like that!' He laughed. 'And I don't believe she'll ever do it again!'".[40]

Hilda Doolittle gave a particularly lively account of the introduction of Jofi in a surreal report on her own encounter with "a little lion-like creature" who approached her while "the Professor" warned her not to get too close because the dog might bite. Doolittle, however, withstood the test:

> "Unintimidated, but distressed by the Professor's somewhat forbidding manner, I not only continued my gestures toward the little chow, but crouched on the floor so that she can snap better if she wants to. Yofi – her name is Yofi – snuggles her nose into my hand and nuzzles her head in delicate sympathy against my shoulders".[41]

The photograph of Freud and his dog in his study is a masterpiece of intuition in as far as it suggests that the test of fear and of readiness to overcome fear revealed not only a patient's relation to the dog but how that patient might feel about the images that dominated Freud's study.

The astonishment at encountering a dog was comparable, that is to say, with the surprise felt upon first seeing Freud's collection. If Freud consistently said nothing of his collection in his published writings, then this was also partly because an assessment of its impact on those who encountered it directly was

39 Cassirer Bernfeld 1953 / 1959, 7th May 1953, I, p. 29.
40 Cassirer Bernfeld 1953 / 1959, 7th May 1953, I, p. 29.
41 Doolittle 1956, p. 148–49.

only by this means to be achieved. Every first-time visitor to Freud's consulting room would be entering a space to which his reaction would itself tell the analyst a good deal – and all the more so when a dog was also present.

The intensity of the love that Freud and Marie Bonaparte felt both for their own and for each other's dogs is attested in the fact that, in 1938, and at a time when his advancing illness was causing him considerable discomfort, Freud agreed to collaborate with his youngest daughter, Anna, on a German translation of Bonaparte's heart-rending book about her own dog, Topsy. This was published in Amsterdam on 12th May.[42] In her foreword to this volume, Anna Freud cites something that her father would often say and which could, incidentally, hardly be more apposite to the scene captured in the photograph taken two years earlier. Freud had pointed up the contrast between the treachery that epitomised mankind and the qualities invariably demonstrated by dogs: the depth of their capacity for trust and the absence of ambiguity in their aggression: "Dogs love their friends and bite their enemies, quite unlike people, who are incapable of pure love and, at every moment, feel the need to blend, and thus disguise, their responses to those they love and to those they loathe".[43] In Marie Bonaparte's photograph of Freud in his study, objects from his collection, aligned on shelves and upon his desk, appear to bear witness to a canine counter-world that is not so very far removed from the realm of art.

For both Freud and Bonaparte, their dogs were more than a source of spiritual solace. As a "vehicle for imagination and projection", they offered the accessible starting point for an intuitive approach to the culture of China, the land of their orign.[44] Hence Freud's particular liking for Chinese figurines, which was indulged especially towards the end of his life. Owing to this interest in the Far East, the geo-cultural range of his collection was greatly enhanced.

4. The legitimacy of the repressed

The mask of an Egyptian mummy visible, in the 1936 photograph, on one of the shelves seen behind Jofi betokens the intense engagement with the history and the culture of Ancient Egypt that was central to Freud's last book: *Moses and Monotheism*. Crucial here was the notion of "the return of that which had been repressed", as a process operating both in the life of a community and in that of the individual.[45] Freud maintained that Moses was himself an Egyptian, and that

42 *Freud and China* 2021, pp. 43, 46.

43 Anna Freud 1981, pp. 9–10.

44 *Freud and China* 2021, p. 47.

45 Sigmund Freud, "Der Mann Moses und die monotheistische Religion", in: *SFG*, vol. 20, p. 342. Cf Bernstein 1998, pp. 69–74; and Schäfer 2003, pp. 9–15.

he had been appointed by the Jews as their own leader in his capacity as a champion of the monotheism espoused by the pharaoh Akhnaten. For the French scholar Jacques Le Rider this thesis signalled Freud's renunciation of the cultural and intellectual legacy of Athens and his return to that of Jerusalem.[46] Yet Freud's collection of idols embodies a diametrically opposed position.[47] For monotheism, with its intolerance of any but a single divinity and its universalising aspirations, is incompatible with the geo-cultural diversity celebrated by the assembled idols.[48] The "return" of a "repressed" polytheism, with universalising aspirations of its own, would not be a reinstated form of religious practice but a symbolic space of liberation.

It is no coincidence that Freud should appear to alternate, in his views and preferences, between a linguistically determined iconoclasm and an intense appreciation for the visual qualities of objects. One finds much the same phenomenon in the case of Franz Kafka.[49] Both Freud and Kafka were well aware that images, however firmly prohibited, suppressed or negated they might be, were nonetheless capable of re-emerging in the form of dreams and nightmares. Through this insight, Freud's approach to psychoanalysis – in its aspiration to resolve identified lapses in behaviour through freeing the imagination – got to the root of the prohibition of images.

The *Moses* of Michelangelo itself validated Freud's method of making the object of his interpretation those repressed images that had defied their own prohibition. It also made clear that this method would itself serve an anti-iconoclastic purpose. In this respect, it could be said that Michelangelo's *Moses* served as a prefiguration of the Freud who would later presume to correct the biblical Moses and to do all he could to ensure that the Mosaic religion give way to science. And, if Freud may be said to have legitimised the use of idols in psychoanalysis, through transforming both his study and his consulting room into a veritable laboratory of images, this occurred in tandem with the emergence and development of his psychoanalytic practice, in which an initial "versatile alertness" would be drawn to one or two items in the collection. Both in the consulting room and in the study, the assembled figures established a resonant space in which images had true agency, in which they were by no means passive, but engaged actively with those encountering them, whose attention they reciprocated.[50]

46 Le Rider 2002.

47 Cf. the commentary on Le Rider's volume by Hartmut Böhme (Böhme 2011, pp. 452–56), which is the starting point for my own contention here.

48 Said 2003.

49 Stadler 2019, pp. 77–94.

50 "Das Entgegenkommende Denken 2015"; on the philosophy of the image act ("*der Bildakt*"): Bredekamp 2015.

Anyone wishing to communicate with Freud within this world of his own creation was required to enter into a space defined by three entities: by himself, by Freud and by the community of idols.

As Hilda Doolittle and other patients and colleagues (such as Binswanger) so memorably reported, it was while surrounded by his collection and with its help that Freud relieved the patient of the images that haunted and troubled him so that these images and the actions compelled by them might in turn become objects of psychoanalytic investigation and treatment. The concern here was to release the images that were buried deep within the individual's psyche, where they were manifest in the form of obsessions and instances of fetishism. An exemplary case in this respect was that of the Wolf Man, in his treatment of whom Freud incorporated a drawing made by the analysand.[51] In so far as the images of unfulfilled desires, of dreams and of fixations could be retrieved, interpreted and thereby neutralised, during the sessions of psychoanalysis, it was assumed that an effective reconciliation between these images and their former victim would follow.[52]

In the light of the spiritualisation that Judaism might be said to have achieved through the prohibition of images, Freud was to accuse Christianity of itself returning to a pantheism almost reminiscent of that of Ancient Egypt: "It was no longer strictly monotheistic, it had adopted numerous symbolic rites from neighbouring peoples, it had reinstated the great Mother Goddess, and it had also found a way to accommodate other figures to be found in polytheistic religions, albeit hierarchically ranked in accordance with their perceived status".[53] Here, however, one can detect Freud pursuing two ostensibly contradictory arguments. On the one hand, he regarded the developments described as a "grave impediment" to spiritualisation; on the other, he emphasised that, from "the point of view of the history of religion" (and, in particular, "the return of that which had been repressed"), Christianity equated to an advance, whereas Judaism would henceforth be, in effect, a fossil.[54] With the help of his collection, Freud nonetheless sought to improve on this outcome, in a process just as pleasing as it was rigorous. And there are few more apposite ways in which Freud might have characterised his collection than to describe it as an element in a process of "transparent

51 Sigmund Freud, "Aus der Geschichte einer infantilen Neurose", in: *SFG*, vol. 16, pp. 111–214, here 132–33. Cf. Blümle 2020, pp. 279–82, with regard to Jacques Lacan.

52 Cf. Gay 1989, p. 18, on that which Freud, regarding his collection, had not admitted: "[...] making peace (or, more humbly, a lasting truce) among id, ego and super ego".

53 Sigmund Freud, "Der Mann Moses und die monotheistische Religion", in: *SFG*, vol. 20, p. 303.

54 Sigmund Freud, "Der Mann Moses und die monotheistische Religion", in: *SFG*, vol. 20, p. 303. Cf. Cacciari 2018, p. 13.

veiling".[55] Freud gave much thought to the dictum, deriving from Mediaeval theology, *credo quia absurdum* (I believe [it] because it is impossible).[56] The insight to which this attests – that it is in contradiction that the truth can be found to reside – might well have served as a motto for his collection. Psychoanalysis, of the sort devised and applied by Freud, albeit ostensibly driven by the spoken word, never entirely lost sight of images.

This state of creative contradiction explains why Freud twice became so intensely preoccupied with Moses to the extent of identifying with him, albeit with two diametrically opposed outcomes. On the first such occasion, between 1901 and 1914, he gradually came to see in Michelangelo's sculpted figure of *Moses* a daring reinterpretation of the biblical account in which this leader of the Jews, when confronted with the evidence of their shameless apostasy, had succeeded in suppressing his own anger and desire for revenge, thereby – as understood in the terminology of Freudian psychoanalysis – achieving a victory for the "ego" over the "id". In the second case, while at work decades later on what was to become his last book, Freud identified Moses as himself an Egyptian and an adherent of monotheism, whom the Jews had, on that account, appointed as their own leader. But they were themselves to prove incapable of adhering to the iconoclastic spirituality to which they had aspired. In assembling and displaying so joyfully diverse a collection of idols, Freud was engaged in a revolt against the severity and illiberality of iconoclasm. As the spaces housing these idols, his study and consulting room at Berggasse were imbued with the spirit of liberation. They can thus also be perceived as the simultaneously physical and intellectual context within which Freud first envisaged the counter-world of his *Moses and Monotheism* and without which that counter-world cannot itself be understood. Much the same relationship prevailed between Freud's seemingly speech-oriented form of psychoanalysis and the rooms – densely packed with so much that might intrigue, seduce or astound the eye – in which it was in practice pursued.

55 This conclusion follows Schäfer 2003, pp. 15–16, 37–38.

56 See, in particular, Sigmund Freud, "Der Mann Moses und die monotheistische Religion", in: *SFG*, vol. 20, p. 300. On the derivation of this dictum: *Wörterbuch der philosophischen Begriffe* 2013, p. 130–31.

CONCLUSION: A NEW TOPICALITY

There are few individuals who, through their intellectual and scientific influence, have left their mark so decisively upon our understanding of humanity – be it the mental state of the individual or the individual's relationship to the community – as has Sigmund Freud. From the very start, however, he was compelled to confront the claim that his own method of psychoanalysis was insufficiently scientific and should, therefore, be replaced by one of a number of alternatives, such as those favoured by empirically inflected psychology. A replacement of just that sort has now largely taken place.[1] As a result, one might well have the impression that Freudian psychoanalysis is today only of retrospective interest, in the context of the history of science.

In fact, psychoanalysis of a Freudian stamp – characterised by the endeavour to grasp and to analyse an underlying pattern of instinctive drives – has repeatedly returned to reaffirm its continuing relevance. It is already clear to what degree a Freudian approach may prove apposite in the age of the Internet, which offers those instinctive drives such scope for expression, so openly and offensively and with an unprecedented frequency, both in social media and on the Dark Web. In view of the now pervasive evidence of a public sphere so infiltrated by something "raw and uncontrollable", it is imperative to insist all the more emphatically on "the difference that psychoanalysis makes: that meticulous process of describing the unconscious structures that underpin a single individual's thinking, feeling and action on the basis of a history of his specific experience of conflict and trauma".[2]

1 On this process: *Forgetting Freud?* 2006.

2 Leuzinger-Bohleber 2021.

Energies of a not entirely unrelated sort infuse the world of images that, every single day, expands through the uploading of digital photographs in heretofore unimaginable quantities.[3] Their essence is the coincidence of the private and the public – itself, in this context, a novelty enabled through technology.[4] The matter of how we now engage with the *image* as a phenomenon – from the ostensibly harmless publication of what is, indisputably, private to the ruthlessness with which formerly taboo motifs are now disseminated – gains an explosive significance when addressed from the point of view of psychoanalysis. Thousands are now employed to comb though new online content in order to filter out all that would appear to contravene legality or to break taboos.[5]

Against such a background, it begins to appear as rather more than a mere philological game to ask, yet again, how Sigmund Freud himself perceived and interpreted the world of images and how he incorporated them within the form of psychoanalysis that he evolved. For it is precisely in this era of the Internet, and the all but infinite access it affords to image worlds potentially no less precarious than enthralling, that such questions have assumed a distinctive new relevance. It is, indeed, possible that Freudian psychoanalysis – on account no less of its intellectual rigour than of the profundity of its engagement with the visual – will find that its best days, as our guide to traversing such an era, are still before it.

3 The photographs recording the installation of the exhibition *Send me an Image* at c/o Berlin in 2021 visualised this most memorably: Erik Kessels, View of his installation "14 HRS in Photos" at the exhibition *Send me an Image*, c/o Berlin, May–September 2021.

4 Bredekamp 2021b.

5 Grassegger & Krause 2016.

BIBLIOGRAPHY

This Bibliography is, in principle, restricted to the original-language version of each item cited and has not, with a few exceptions, been further extended through the addition of pre-existing English translations of texts originating in other languages.

Where several publications by the same author are cited, these appear in chronological order of first publication.

Sigmund Freud is himself the focus of a four-part segment within the overall listing. This comprises:

1. publications devoted to Freud in connection with one or more of the chief themes addressed in the present volume;
2. editions of Freud's notebooks and diaries;
3. editions of Freud's correspondence;
4. those of Freud's own works that are here of particular significance. Items included in each segment are listed in chronological order.

Allgemeines Lexikon der bildenden Künstler von der Antike bis zur Gegenwart, est. Ullrich Thieme & Felix Becker, vols 1–37, Leipzig, 1992

Alt, Peter-André, *Sigmund Freud. Der Arzt der Moderne. Eine Biographie*, Munich 2016

Andreas-Salomé, Lou, *In der Schule bei Freud. Tagebuch eines Jahres (1912/13)*, Frankfurt am Main 1983

Andreas-Salomé, Lou, *Das "zweideutige" Lächeln der Erotik. Texte zur Psychoanalyse*, Freiburg 1990

Anzieu, Didier, *L'auto-analyse de Freud et la découverte de la psychanalyse*, 2 vols, Paris 1975

Armstrong, Richard H., "From Iconography to Archeology. Freud after Charcot", *American Imago*, LXXVIII / 2 (2021), pp. 215–43

Armstrong, Richard H., Miriam Leonard & Daniel Orrells, "Freud's Antiquity: Between Object and Ideal", in: *Freud's Antiquity: Object / Idea / Desire*, exh. cat., ed. Richard H. Armstrong, Miriam Leonard, Daniel Orrells, Tom DeRose & Karolina Heller, London 2023

Assmann, Jan, *Moses der Ägypter. Entzifferung einer Gedächtnisspur*, Munich 1998

Assmann, Jan, "Der Fortschritt in der Geistigkeit. Sigmund Freuds Konstruktion des Judentums", *Psyche*, LVI (2002), pp. 154–71

Assmann, Jan, *Exodus. Die Revolution der Alten Welt*, Munich 2019

Aurnhammer, Achim & Ralf von den Hoff, "Arthur Schnitzler und die Kunst der Antike", in: *Arthur Schnitzler und die bildende Kunst*, ed. Achim Aurnhammer & Ralf von den Hoff, Baden-Baden 2021

Barth, Thomas, *Wer Freud Ideen gab. Eine systematische Untersuchung*, Münster, New York, Munich & Berlin 2013

Benthien, Claudia, *Barockes Schweigen. Rhetorik und Performativität des Sprachlosen im 17. Jahrhundert*, Paderborn & Munich 2006

Bergson, Henri, *L'Évolution créatrice*, Paris 1907

Bergstein, Mary, "Freud's 'Moses of Michelangelo'. Vasari, Photography, and Art Historical Practice", *The Art Bulletin*, LXXXVIII / 1 (2006), pp. 158–76

Bergstein, Mary, *Mirrors of Memory. Freud, Photography, and the History of Art*, Ithaca, NY, & London 2010

Bernfeld, Siegfried & Suzanne Cassirer Bernfeld, *Bausteine der Freud-Biographik*, ed. & trans. Ilse Grubrich-Simitis, Frankfurt am Main 1988

Bernheim, Hippolyte, *De la suggestion et de son application à la thérapeutique*, Paris 1887

Bernheim, Hippolyte, *Die Suggestion und ihre Heilwirkung*, trans. Sigmund Freud, Leipzig & Vienna 1888

Bernstein, Richard J., *Freud and the Legacy of Moses*, Cambridge 1998

Holy Bible (King James Version, 1611), London & New York 1922

Biemann, Asher D., *Michelangelo und die jüdische Moderne*, Göttingen & Vienna 2016

Binswanger, Ludwig, *Erinnerungen an Sigmund Freud*, Bern 1956

Binswanger, Ludwig & Aby Warburg, *Die unendliche Heilung. Aby Warburgs Krankengeschichte*, ed. Chantal Marazia & Davide Stimilli, Zürich & Berlin 2007

Blum, Gerd, "Michelangelo als Neuer Mose. Zur Rezeptionsgeschichte von Michelangelos Moses. Vasari, Nietzsche, Freud, Thomas Mann", *Zeitschrift für Ästhetik und Allgemeine Kunstwissenschaft*, LIII / 1 (2008), pp. 73–106

Blum, Gerd, "'In foramine petrae'. Michelangelos wörtliche Auslegung der Vulgata und die Hörner seines Moses in San Pietro in Vincoli", *Vulgata in Dialogue*, IV (2020), pp. 45–78

Blümle, Claudia, "'La dolce vita'. Lacans film- und bildtechnische Umwelten", in: *Milieu Fragmente. Technologische und ästhetische Perspektiven*, ed. Rebekka Ladewig & Angelika Seppi, Leipzig 2020

Böhme, Hartmut, *Fetischismus und Kultur. Eine andere Theorie der Moderne*, Reinbek bei Hamburg 2006

Böhme, Hartmut, "Die Antike 'nach' Freud", in: *Freud und die Antike*, ed. Claudia Benthien, Hartmut Böhme & Inge Stephan, Göttingen 2011, pp. 423–56

Bourgeois, Louise, "Freud's Toys", *Artforum*, XVIII / 5 (1990), pp. 116–18

Bredekamp, Horst, "Denkende Hände. Überlegungen zur Bildkunst der Naturwissenschaft", in: *Von der Wahrnehmung zur Erkenntnis. From Perception to Understanding. Symposium der Schering Forschungsgesellschaft zur Ehren von Professor Dr. Dr. h.c. Günter Stock, Februar 2004*, ed. Monika Lessl & Jürgen Mittelstrass, Berlin & Heidelberg 2005, pp. 109–32

Bredekamp, Horst, "Michelangelos Moses als Gedankenfilm. Freuds Ambivalenz gegenüber der Kinematographie", in: *Kino im Kopf. Psychologie und Film seit Sigmund Freud*, exh. cat., ed. Kristina Jaspers & Wolf Unterberger, Berlin 2006, pp. 31–37

Bredekamp, Horst, *Der Bildakt. Frankfurter Adorno-Vorlesungen 2007*, Berlin 2015

Bredekamp, Horst, *Aby Warburg, der Indianer. Berliner Erkundungen einer liberalen Ethnologie*, Berlin 2019

Bredekamp, Horst, *Michelangelo*, Berlin 2021a

Bredekamp, Horst, *Bild, Recht, Zeit. Ein Plädoyer für die Neugewinnung von Distanz*, Munich 2021b

Bredekamp, Horst, "Inverse Freunde. Aby Warburg und Sigmund Freud: Ablehnung und Seelenverwandtschaft", in: *Das Subversive Bild. Festschrift für Jürgen Müller*, ed.

Bertram Kaschek, Teresa Ende, Jan-David Mentzel & Frank Schmidt, Berlin 2022, pp. 385–96

Breger, Louis, *Freud. Darkness in the Midst of Vision*, New York, Chichester & Weinheim 2000

Briefel, Aviva, "Sacred Objects / Illusory Idols. The Fake in Freud's 'The Moses of Michelangelo'", *American Imago*, LX / 1 (2003), pp. 21–40

Cacciari, Massimo, *Icone della legge*, Milan 1985

Carroy, Jacqueline, "Vorwort", in: Lydia Marinelli, *Psyches Kanon. Zur Publikationsgeschichte rund um den Internationalen Psychoanalytischen Verlag*, Vienna & Berlin 2009, pp. 7–10

Cassirer Bernfeld, Suzanne, "Freud and Archeology", *The American Imago*, VIII / 2 (June 1951), pp. 107–28

Cassirer Bernfeld, Suzanne, Interviews 1953 / 1959 (manuscript), in: Sigmund Freud Papers, Library of Congress, Washington, D. C., Box 126, folder 12

Cicognara, Leopoldo, *Storia della scultura dal suo risorgimento in Italia fino al secolo di Canova*, 2nd edn, vol. V, Prato 1824

Clair, Jean, Cathrin Pichler & Wolfgang Pichler, *Wunderblock. Eine Geschichte der modernen Seele*, exh. cat., ed. Elisabeth Madlener, Vienna 1989

Clair, Jean, "Freud: l'idole et la parole", in: *Sigmund Freud. Du regard à l'écoute*, exh. cat., ed. Jean Clair, Paris 2018, pp. 18–37

Clark, Ronald W. *Freud: the Man and the Cause*, London 1980

Condivi, Ascanio, *Vita di Michelangelo Buonarroti*, Rome 1553

Die Couch. Vom Denken im Liegen, ed. Lydia Marinelli, Munich, Berlin, London, New York 2006

Crary, Jonathan, *Suspensions of Perception: Attention, Spectacle and Modern Culture*, Cambridge, Mass., 2000

Cremerius, Johannes "S. Freud – Ein grosser Verhüller", *Neue Rundschau*, LXXXII / 1 (1971), pp. 187–91

Cremerius, Johannes, "Freud bei der Arbeit über die Schulter geschaut. Seine Technik im Spiegel von Schülern und Patienten", in: *Humanität und Technik in der Psychoanalyse. Festschrift für Gerhart Scheunert zum 75. Geburtstag (Jahrbuch der Psychoanalyse*, supplement 6), Bern, Stuttgart & Vienna 1981, pp. 123–58

Cremerius, Johannes, *Vom Handwerk des Psychoanalytikers. Das Werkzeug der psychoanalytischen Technik*, 2 vols, Stuttgart – Bad Canstatt 1984

D'Agata, Anna Lucia, "Sigmund Freud and Aegean Archeology. Mycenaean and Cypriote Material from his Collection of Antiquities", *Studi Micenei ed Egeo-Anatolico*, XXXII (1974), pp. 7–41

D'Angelo, Marina, *"So will ich nur entfliehen". Sigmund Freuds Italienreisen*, Giessen 2020

Davies, Erica, "'Eine Welt wie im Traum'. Freuds Antikensammlung", in: *"Meine ... alten und dreckigen Götter". Aus Sigmund Freuds Sammlung*, exh. cat., ed. Lydia Marinelli, Vienna 1998, pp. 94–101

Deicher, Suzanne, "Mikroskopische Bilder der Nervensysteme in Sigmund Freuds [...] der 70er und 80er Jahre", in: *Bildwelten des Wissens. Kunsthistorisches Jahrbuch für Bildkritik*, II / 2 (2004), pp. 29–39

Deleuze, Gilles, *Cinéma, 1: l'image-mouvement*, Paris 1983

Dennis, George, *The Cities and Cemetries of Etruria*, 2 vols, London 1878

Didi-Huberman, Georges, *Erfindung der Hysterie. Die photographische Klinik von Jean-Martin Charcot*, Munich 1997

Didi-Hubermnan, Georges, *L'image survivante. Histoire de l'art et temps des fantômes selon Aby Warburg*, Paris 2002a

Didi-Huberman, Georges, "The Surviving Image. Aby Warburg and Tylorian Anthropology", *Oxford Art Journal*, XXV / 1 (2002b), pp. 59–70

Didi-Huberman, Georges, *Das Nachleben der Bilder. Kunstgeschichte und Phantomzeit nach Aby Warburg*, trans. Michael Bischoff, Berlin 2010

Dissimilazione onesta oder Die ehrliche Verstellung. Von der Weisheit der versteckten Beunruhigung in Wort, Bild und Tat. Martin Warnke zu Ehren. Ein Symposium, ed. Horst Bredekamp, Michael Diers, Ruth Tesmar, Franz-Joachim Verspohl, Hamburg 2007

Doane, Mary Ann, *The Emergence of Cinematic Time. Modernity, Contingency, the Archive*, Cambridge, Mass., & London 2002

Dohmen, Christoph, "Nuntii personarum et rerum. Mose, das leuchtende Angesicht der Tora", *Biblica*, LXXXVI / 4 (2005), pp. 583–91

Doolittle, Hilda [as H. D.], *Tribute to Freud*, New York 1956

Einem, Herbert von, "Unvollendetes und Unvollendbares im Werk Michelangelos", in: *Torso – Das unvollendete als künstlerische Form: Ein Symposion*, ed. Josef A. Schmoll gen. Eisenwerth, Bern & Munich 1959, pp. 69–82

Engelman, Edmund, *Berggasse 19. Das Wiener Domizil Sigmund Freuds*, Stuttgart & Zürich 1977a

Engelman, Edmund, "Ruckbild", in: *Edmund Engelman. Berggasse 19. Das Wiener Domizil Sigmund Freuds*, Stuttgart & Zürich 1977b, pp. 51–64

Engelman, Edmund, *Siegmund Freud, Wien IX, Berggasse 19*, Vienna 1993

Das Entgegenkommende Denken. Verstehen zwischen Form und Empfindung, ed. Franz Engel & Sabine Marienberg, Berlin & Boston 2015

Ernst, Werner W., "'Das Unbehagen in der Kultur' und die Religion", in: *"Unbehagen in der Kultur" – Variationen zu Sigmund Freuds Kultukritik*, ed. Herbert Bickel & Helmwart Hierdeis, Vienna, Berlin & Münster 2008, pp. 143–51

Ernst, Werner W., *Das Böse, die Trennung und der Tod. Eine Theorie des Bösen*, Vienna 2014

Ernst, Werner W., "'Totem und Tabu' und der christliche Opferbegriff", in: *Von Ödipus zu Eichmann. Kulturanthropologische Voraussetzungen von Gewalt*, ed. Dietmar Regensburger & Christian Wessely, Marburg 2015, pp. 59–70

Fehrenbach, Frank, *Quasi Vivo. Lebendigkeit in italienischen Kunst der Frühen Neuzeit*, Berlin & Boston 2021

Forgetting Freud? For a New Historiography of Psychoanalysis, special issue of *Science in Context*, XIX / 1 (2006)

Forrester, John, "Freudsches Sammeln", in: *"Meine ... alten und dreckigen Götter"*, exh. cat., ed. Lydia Marinelli, Vienna 1998, pp. 20–35

Freud, Anna, "Vorwort zur Neuausgabe", in: Marie Bonaparte, *Topsy. Der goldhaarige Chow*, trans. Anna Freud & Sigmund Freud, Frankfurt am Main 1981, pp. 7–10

Freud, Martin, *Mein Vater Sigmund Freud*, Heidelberg 1999

FREUD, SIGMUND: 1. his collection / his library / and Antiquity

Engelman, Edmund, *Berggasse 19. Das Wiener Domizil Sigmund Freuds*, Stuttgart & Zürich 1977a

Sigmund Freud. Sein Leben in Bildern und Texten, ed. Ernst Freud, Lucie Freud & Ilse Grubrich-Simitis, Frankfurt am Main 1985

Excavations and Their Objects. Freud's Collection of Antiquity, ed. Stephen Barker, Albany, NY, 1996

"Meine ... alten und dreckigen Götter". Aus Sigmund Freuds Sammlung, exh. cat., ed. Lydia Marinelli, Vienna 1998

Sigmund Freud and Art. His Personal Collection of Antiquities, exh. cat., ed. Lynn Gamwell & Richard Wells, New York & London 1989

Freud as Collector, exh. cat., ed. Nicholas Reeves & Yumiko Ueno, Tokyo 1996

Freud's Library. A Comprehensive Catalogue / Freuds Bibliothek. Vollständiger Katalog, ed. J. Keith Davies & Gerhard Fichter, London & Tübingen 2006
Freud's Sculpture, exh. cat., ed. Penelope Curtis & Jon Wood, Leeds 2006
Janine Burke, *The Gods of Freud. Sigmund Freud's Art Collection*, Sydney, New York & Toronto 2006
Freud und die Antike, ed. Claudia Benthien, Hartmut Böhme & Inge Stephan, Göttingen 2011
Freud and the Rings, exh. cat., ed. Morag Wilhelm, Jerusalem 2018
Freud, Berggasse 19. Ursprungsort der Psychoanalyse, ed. Monika Pessler & Daniela Finzi, Berlin 2020
Freud and China. Possession and Imagination, exh. cat., ed. Craig Clunas, London 2021
Freud's Antiquity: Object / Idea / Desire, exh. cat., ed. Richard H. Armstrong, Miriam Leonard, Daniel Orrells, Tom DeRose & Karolina Heller, London 2023
Innenwelten. Sigmund Freud und die Kunst, exh. cat., ed. Nicole Fritz & Monika Pessler, Tübingen & Cologne 2023

FREUD, SIGMUND: 2. notebooks / diaries
Sigmund Freud: Aus den Anfängen der Psychoanalyse. Briefe an Wilhelm Fliess, Abhandlungen und Notizen aus den Jahren 1887–1902, ed. Marie Bonaparte, Anna Freud & Ernst Kris, London 1950
Sigmund Freud: Tagebuch 1929–1939. Kürzeste Chronik, ed. Michael Molnar & Christfried Tögel, Basel & Frankfurt am Main 1996
Sigmund Freud: Notizbücher 1901–1936, ed. Albrecht Hirschmüller & Christfried Tögel, on the basis of material prepared by Gerhard Fichtner & Marina D'Angelo, Tübingen & Lausanne 2021; 2nd edn Berlin & Vienna 2024
(also available online at: http://www.freud-bibliographik.de/Freuds%20Notizbuecher%20 1901-1936%20-%204.%Fassung.pdf)

FREUD, SIGMUND: 3. correspondence
Sigmund Freud: Briefe 1873–1939, sel. & ed. Ernst L. Freud & Lucie Freud, 2nd edn Frankfurt am Main 1968
Freud / Jung 1974:
Sigmund Freud und C. G. Jung: Briefwechsel, ed. William McGuire & Wolfgang Sauerländer, Frankfurt am Main 1974
Freud / Abraham 1980:
Sigmund Freud und Karl Abraham: Briefe 1907–1926, ed. Hilda C. Abraham & Ernst L. Freud, Frankfurt am Main 1980
Freud / Fliess 1986:
Sigmund Freud: Briefe an Wilhelm Fliess 1887–1904, ed. Jeffrey Mousaieff Masson, Michael Schröter & Gerhard Fichtner, Frankfurt am Main 1986
Freud / Binswanger 1992:
Sigmund Freud und Ludwig Binswanger: Briefwechsel 1908–1938, ed. Gerhard Fichtner, Frankfurt am Main 1992
Freud / Ferenczi 1993:
Sigmund Freud und Sándor Ferenczi: Briefwechsel, vol. I/2: *1912–1914*, ed. Eva Brabant, Ernst Falzender & Patrizia Giampieri-Deutsch, Vienna, Cologne & Weimar 1993
Freud / Ernest Jones 1993:
The Complete Correspondence of Sigmund Freud and Ernest Jones 1908–1939, ed. R. Andrew Paskauskas, intr. Riccardo Steiner, Cambridge, Mass., & London 1993
Freud / travel letters 2003:

Sigmund Freud: Unser Herz zeigt nach dem Süden. Reisebriefe 1895–1923, ed. Christfried Tögel, with the assistance of Michael Molnar, Berlin 2003

Freud / Martha Bernays 2011 / 2013 / 2015 / 2019:

Sigmund Freud und Martha Bernays: Die Brautbriefe, ed. Gerhard Fichtner, Ilse Grubrich-Simitis & Albrecht Hirschmüller, 4 vols Frankfurt am Main 2011 (*Juni 1882–Juli 1883*), 2013 (*Juli 1883–Dezember 1883*), 2015 (*Januar 1884–September 1884*), 2019 (*September 1884–August 1885*)

Freud / Marie Bonaparte 2022:

Marie Bonaparte et Sigmund Freud: Correspondance intégrale 1925–1939, ed. Rémy Amouroux; trans. Olivier Manonni, Paris 2022

FREUD, SIGMUND: 4. his own publications that are here of particular significance

Freud, Sigmund (anonymously), "Der Moses des Michelangelo", *Imago*, III / 1 (April 1914), pp. 15–36

Freud, Sigmund, *Zur Psychopathologie des Alltagslebens. Über Vergessen, Versprechen, Vergreifen, Aberglaube und Irrtum*, 5th enl. edn Berlin 1917

Freud, Sigmund, "Der Moses des Michelangelo", in: *Gesammelte Schriften*, vol. X, ed. Anna Freud, Otto Rank, Adolf J. Storfer, Leipzig, Vienna & Zürich 1924, pp. 257–86

Freud, Sigmund, "Nachtrag zur Arbeit über den Moses des Michelangelo", *Imago*, XIII / 2–4 (1927), pp. 552–53

Freud, Sigmund, "Notiz über den 'Wunderblock'", in: *Sigmund Freud. Gesammelte Werke*, vol. XIV: *Werke aus den Jahren 1925–1931*, ed. Anna Freud, in collaboration with Marie Bonaparte, London 1948, pp. 3–8

Freud, Sigmund, "Der Wahn und die Träume in W. Jensens *Gradiva*", in: *Sigmund Freud: Studienausgabe*, vol. X: *Bildende Kunst und Literatur*, ed. Alexander Mitscherlich, Angela Richards & James Strachey, Frankfurt am Main 1969a, pp. 9–85

Freud, Sigmund, "Der Moses des Michelangelo", in: *Sigmund Freud. Studienausgabe*, vol. X: *Bildende Kunst und Literatur*, ed. Alexander Mitscherlich, Angela Richards & James Strachey, Frankfurt am Main 1969b, pp. 195–222

Freud, Sigmund, "Eine Kindheitserinnerrung des Leonardo da Vinci", in: *Sigmund Freud. Studienausgabe*, vol. X: *Bildende Kunst und Literatur*, ed. Alexander Mitscherlich, Angela Richards & James Strachey, Frankfurt am Main 1969c, pp. 87–159

Freud, Sigmund, "Zur Einleitung der Behandlung (Weitere Ratschläge zur Technik der Psychoanalyse I)" (1913), in: *Sigmund Freud. Studienausgabe, Ergänzungsband: Schriften zur Behandlungstechnik*, ed. Alexander Mitscherlich, Angela Richards, James Strachey & Ilse Grubrich-Simitis, Frankfut am Main 2000, pp. 181–203

Freud-Marlé, Lilly, *Mein Onkel Sigmund Freud. Erinnerungen an eine grosse Familie*, ed. Christfried Tögel, Berlin 2006

Friedberg, Anna, "An *Unheimlich* Maneuver between Psychoanalysis and the Cinema. Secrets of a Soul (1926)", in: *The Films of G. W. Pabst. An Extraterritorial Cinema*, ed. Eric Rentschler, New Brunswick., NJ, & London 1990, pp. 41–51

Frommel, Christoph Luitpold (in collaboration with Maria Forcellino, Claudia Echinger-Maurach & Antonio Forcellino), *Michelangelo – Marmor und Geist. Das Grabmal Papst Julius' II. und seine Statuen*, Regensburg 2014

Fuller, Peter, *Art and Psychoanalysis*, London 1980

Fuss, Diana, *The Sense of an Interieur*, New York 2004

Gallo, Rubén, "Freud's Mexican Antiquities. Psychoanalysis and Human Sacrifice", *October*, CXXXV (2011), pp. 70–92

Galst, Jay and Peter van Alfen, *Ophthalmologia Optica & Visio in Nummis*, Piribebuy & New York 2013

Gamwell, Lynn, "The Origins of Freud's Antiquities Collection", in: *Sigmund Freud and Art. His Personal Collection of Antiquities*, exh. cat., ed. Lynn Gamwell & Richard Wells, New York & London 1989, pp. 20–32

Gamwell, Lynn, "A Collector Analyses Collecting. Sigmund Freud on the Passion to Possess", in: *Excavations and their Objects. Freud's Collection of Antiquity*, ed. Stephen Barker, Albany, NY, 1996, pp. 1–2

Gardiner, Muriel, *Der Wolfsmann / vom Wolfsmann. Mit der Krankengeschichte des Wolfsmannes von Sigmund Freud, dem Nachtrag von Ruth Mack Brunswick und einem Vorwort von Anna Freud*, Frankfurt am Main 1972

Gay, Peter, "Zum Gedenken am Sigmund Freud", in: *Edmund Engelmann, Berggasse 19. Das Wiener Domizil Sigmund Freuds*, Stuttgart & Zürich 1977, pp. 5–49

Gay, Peter, "Introduction", in: *Sigmund Freud and His Art. His Personal Collection of Antiquities*, exh. cat., ed. Lynn Gamwell & Richard Wells, New York & London 1980, pp. 15–19

Gay, Peter, *A Godless Jew: Freud, atheism and the making of psychoanalysis*, New York & London 1987

Gay, Peter, *Freud: A Life for Our Time*, London 1988

Germer, Kerstin, "'Der Fortschritt in der Geistigkeit'. Schönbergs Oper *Moses und Aron* in der Perspektive von Freuds Moses-Studie", in: *Erzeugen und Nachvollziehen von Sinn. Rationale, performative und mimetische Verstehensbegriffe in den Kulturwissenschaften*, ed. Martin Zenck & Markus Jüngling, Munich 2011, pp. 331–44

Ginzburg, Carlo, "Spie. Radici di un paradigma indiziario", in: *Crisi della ragione. Nuovi modelli nel rapporto tra sapere e attività umana*, ed. Aldo Gargani, 2nd edn Turin 1980, pp. 57–106

Gombrich, Ernst, "Freud's Aesthetics", in: *Tributes: interpreters of our cultural tradition*, Oxford 1984, pp. 93–115

Grassegger, Hannes & Till Krause, "Inside Facebook. Im Netz des Bösen", *Süddeutsche Zeitung Magazin*, no. 50 (15 December 2016), pp. 14–23

Greenblatt, Stephen & Adam Phillips, *Second Chances: Shakespeare and Freud*, New Haven & London 2024

Grimm, Herman, *Leben Michelangelo's*, 2 vols, Hanover 1860, 1863

Grimm, Herman, *Leben Michelangelos*, ed. Ludwig Goldscheider, no. loc 1953

Grubrich-Simitis, Ilse, *Zurück zu Freuds Texten. Stumme Dokumente sprechen machen*, Frankfurt am Main 1993

Grubrich-Simitis, Ilse, *Michelangelos Moses und Freuds "Wagstuck". Eine Collage*, Frankfurt am Main 2004

Gsell Fels, Theodor, *Rom und die Campagna*, 7th edn Leipzig & Vienna 1912

Guderian, Claudia, *Die Couch in der Psychoanalyse. Geschichte und Gegenwart von Setting und Raum*, Giessen 2018

Handler Spitz, Ellen, "Psychoanalysis and the Legacies of Antiquity", in: *Sigmund Freud and Art. His Personal Collection of Antiquities*, exh. cat., ed. Lynn Gamwell & Richard Wells, New York & London 1989, pp. 152–71

Harmat, Pál, "Sigmund Freud the Art Smuggler", *Budapest Review of Books*, IV (1994), pp. 190–92

Heckscher, William S., "Die Genesis der Ikonologie", in: *Ikonographie und Ikonologie. Theorien – Entwicklung – Probleme*, ed. Ekkehard Kaemmerling, Cologne 1984, pp. 112–64

Herding, Klaus, *Freuds Leonardo. Eine Auseinandersetzung mit psychoanalytischen Theorien der Gegenwart*, Munich 1998

Herzog, Dagmar, *Cold War Freud. Psychoanalyse in einem Zeitalter der Katastrophen*, Berlin 2023

Hirschmüller, Albrecht & Christfried Tögel, "Gedankensplitter – Gedankenkeime. Freuds Notizbüchlein aus den Jahren 1901 bis 1936", in: *Sigmund Freud: Notizbücher 1901–1936*, ed. Albrecht Hirschmüller & Christfried Tögel, Tübingen & Lausanne 2021; 2nd edn Berlin & Vienna 2024

Huizinga, Johan, *Homo ludens. Versuch einer Bestimmung des Spielelementes der Kultur*, Basel, Brussels, Cologne & Vienna 1938

(originally published as: *Homo ludens: Proeve eener bepaling van het spelement der cultuur*, Haarlem 1938)

Jäger, Felix, "Suggestive Materials. Constructing Cure in Freud's Collection", in: *Bildersammlungen als Denkmaterial. Materialismus, Realismus, Kunst (1900–1960)*, ed. Carolin Behrmann & Steffen Haug, Berlin 2023

Jahnke, Selma, "I primi diari di Ludwig Pollak e l'autobiografia (1924) di Sigmund Freud. Percorsi paralleli nella formazione di Ludwig Pollak e di Sigmund Freud come documento di una orizonte generazionale e di un *milieu* comune", in: *Ludwig Pollak. Archeologo e mercante d'arte. Praga 1868–Auschwitz 1943. Gli anni d'oro del collezionismo internazionale da Giovanni Barracco a Sigmund Freud*, ed. Orietta Rossini, Rome 2018, pp. 121–31

Jensen, Uffa, *Wie die Couch nach Kalkutta kam. Eine Globalgeschichte der frühen Psychoanalyse*, Berlin 2019

Jensen, Wilhelm, "Gradiva. Ein pompejanisches Phantasiestück", in: *Der Wahn und die Träume in W. Jensens "Gradiva", mit dem Text der Erzählung von Wilhelm Jensen*, ed. Bernd Urban & Johannes Cremerius, Frankfurt am Main 1973, pp. 21–86

Jones, Ernest, *Sigmund Freud: Life and Work*, vol. I: *The Young Freud: 1856–1900*, London 1953

Jones, Ernest, *Sigmund Freud: Life and Work*, vol. II: *Years of Maturity: 1901–1919*, London 1955

Jones, Ernest, *Sigmund Freud: Life and Work*, vol. III: *The Last Phase: 1919–1939*, London, 1957

Kämpf, Tobias, "Le pape émule du prohète", in *Moïse, figures d'un prophète*, exh. cat., ed. Anne Hélène Hoog, Matthieu Somon & Matthieu Léglise, Paris 2015, pp. 86–95

Karsten, Arne, *Der Untergang der Welt von gestern. Wien und die K. u. K. Monarchie 1911–1919*, Munich 2019

Keel, Othmar, *Die Weisheit spielt vor Gott. Ein ikonographischer Beitrag zur Deutung des Mesahäqät in Sprüche 8, 30 f.*, Freiburg & Göttingen 1974

Kessler, Frank, "Henri Bergson und die Kinematographie", in: *Theorien zum frühen Kino*, ed. Frank Kessler, Sabine Lenk & Martin Loiperdinger (*KINtop. Jahrbuch zur Erforschung des frühen Films* 12), Frankfurt am Main & Basel 2003, pp. 12–16

Kogel, Jörg-Dieter, *Im Land der Träume. Mit Sigmund Freud in Italien*, Berlin 2019

Köhler, Thomas, *Freuds Schriften zu Literatur, Kunst und Ästhetik. Eine Darstellung und kritische Bewertung*, Giessen 2014

Kolbrener, William, "Death of Moses Revisited. Repetition and Creative Memory in Freud and the Rabbis", *American Imago*, LXVII / 2 (2010), pp. 243–62

Kraus, Karl, "Von den Nachdenklichen und den Betriebsamen", *Die Fackel*, XV / 395–397 (28th March 1914), p. 57

Kuspit, Donald, "A Mighty Metaphor. The Analogy of Archeology and Psychoanalysis", in: *Sigmund Freud and Art. His Personal Collection of Antiquities*, exh. cat., ed. Lynn Gamwell & Richard Wells, New York & London 1989, pp. 133–51

Le Rider, Jacques, *Freud, de l'Acropole au Sinaï: Le retour à l'Antique des Modernes viennois*, Paris 2002

Lermolieff, Ivan (= Giovanni Morelli), *Kunstkritische Studien über italienische Malerei. Die Galerien Borghese und Doria Panfili in Rom*, Leipzig 1890

Leroux, Georges, "'Saxa loquuntur': l'archéologie de Freud", in: *Penser Freud avec Patrick Mahoney*, ed. Louise Grenier & Isabelle Lasvergnas, Montreal 2004, pp. 121–54

Leuzinger-Bohleber, Marianne, "Wo bleibt die dritte Aufklärung?", *Frankfurter Allgemeine Zeitung*, no. 263, 11 November 2021, p. 8

Liebenwein, Wolfgang, *Studiolo. Die Entstehung eines Raumtyps und seine Entwicklung bis um 1600*, West Berlin 1977

Lloyd, William Watkiss, *The Moses of Michel Angelo. A Study of Art, History and Legend*, London 1863

Loewenberg, Peter, "The Pagan Freud", in: *Excavations and their Objects. Freud's Collection of Antiquity*, ed. Stephen Barker, Albany, NY, 1996, pp. 13–32

Maciejewski, Franz, *Der Moses der Sigmund Freud. Ein unheimlicher Bruder*, Göttingen 2006

Macmillan, Malcolm & Peter J. Swales, "Observations from the Refuse-Heap. Freud, Michelangelo's *Moses*, and Psychoanalysis", *American Imago*, LX / 1 (2003), pp. 41–104

Manow, Philip, *Politische Ursprungsphantasien. Der Leviathan und sein Erbe*, Konstanz 2011

Marinelli, Lydia, "'Meine... alten und dreckigen Götter'. Aus Sigmund Freuds Sammlung", in: *"Meine... alten und dreckigen Götter". Aus Sigmund Freuds Sammlung*, exh. cat., ed. Lydia Marinelli, Vienna 1998, pp. 9–19

Marinelli, Lydia, "Vorstellungen eines Möbels", in: *Die Couch. Vom Denken im Liegen*, ed. Lydia Marinelli, Munich, Berlin, London and New York 2006, pp. 7–29

Marinelli, Lydia, *Psyches Kanon. Zur Publikationsgeschichte rund um den Internationalen Psychoanalytischen Verlag*, Vienna & Berlin 2009

Mastroianni, Giovanni, "Il buon Dio di Aby Warburg", *Belfagor*, LV / 4 (2000), pp. 413–42

Mayer, Andreas, "'Ein Übermass an Gefälligkeit'. Der Sammler Jean-Martin Charcot und sein Objekte", in: *"Meine ... alten und dreckigen Götter". Aus Sigmund Freud's Sammlung*, exh. cat., ed. Lydia Marinelli, Vienna 1998, p. 46–59

Mayer, Andreas, "Objektwelten des Unbewussten. Fakten und Fetische in Charcots Museum und Freuds Behandlungspraxis", in: *Sammeln als Wissen. Das Sammeln und seine wissenschaftsgeschichtliche Bedeutung*, ed. Anke te Heesen & E.C. Spary, Göttingen 2001, pp. 169–98

Mayer, Andreas, *Mikroskopie der Psyche. Die Anfänge der Psychoanalyse im Hypnose-Labor*, Göttingen 2002

Mayer, Andreas, "*Gradiva* rediviva. Ein Bewegungsbild zwischen Wissenschaft und Phantasie", in: *Freud und die Antike*, ed. Claudia Benthien, Hartmut Böhme & Inge Stephan, Göttingen 2011, pp. 117–42

Mayer, Andreas, "Freud à Paris: Souvenirs du Musée Charcot", in: *Sigmund Freud. Du regard à l'écoute*, exh. cat., ed. Jean Clair, Paris 2018, pp. 51–59

Mayer, Heike, "Schweigen", in: *Historisches Wörterbuch der Rhetorik*, ed. Gert Ueding, vol. VIII, Darmstadt 2007, cols. 686–706

Merkel Guldan, Margarete, *Die Tagebücher von Ludwig Pollak: Kennerschaft und Kunthandel in Rom 1893–1934*, Vienna 1988

Metken, Günter, *Spurensicherung. Kunst als Anthropologie und Selbstforschung. Fiktive Wissenschaften in der heutigen Kunst*, Cologne 1977

Molnar, Michael, "Die Abendteuerlust des Sammelns", in: *"Meine… alten und dreckigen Götter". Aus Sigmund Freuds Sammlung*, exh. cat., ed. Lydia Marinelli, Vienna 1998, pp. 36–45

Molnar, Michael, "Half-Way Region", in: *Freud's Sculpture*, exh. cat., ed. Penelope Curtis & Jon Wood, Leeds 2006, pp. 19–26

Molnar, Michael, "From Image to Evidence. 'At the Historic Corner Window. 17. 6. 1897'", *Visual Resources. An International Journal on Images and their Uses*, XXIII / 1–2 (2007), pp. 119–27 (= special issue, ed. Mary Bergstein, on *Visual Documentation in Freud's Vienna*)

Molnar, Michael, "Freud in the National Portrait Gallery", *American Imago*, LXIX / 1 (2012), pp. 107–33

Money-Kyrle, Roger E., "Looking backwards – and forwards", *International Review of Psycho-Analysis*, VI (1979), pp. 265–72

Montserrat, Dominic, "Freud and the Archaeology of Aspiration", *Apollo*, CLIV / 473 (2001), pp. 27–34

Moreau Ricaud, Michelle, *Freud collectionneur*, Paris 2011

Morelli, Giovanni, (Ivan Lermolieff), *Della pittura italiana. Studii storico critici. Le Gallerie Borghese e Doria Pamphili in Roma*, Milan 1897

Moser-Ernst, Sybille, & Ursula Marinelli, "Das Goldene Kalb und andere Objektbeziehungen", in: *Im Drama des Lebens Gott begegnen. Einblicke in die Theologie Józef Niewiandomskis*", ed. Nikolaus Wandinger & Petra Steinmair Pösel, Vienna & Münster 2011, pp. 533–59

Mühlleitner, Elke (with the assistance of Johannes Reichmayr), *Biographisches Lexikon der Psychoanalyse. Die Mitglieder der Psychologischen Mittwoch-Gesellschaft und der Wiener Psychoanalytischen Vereinigung von 1902–1938*, Tübingen 1992

Müller, Lothar, *Freuds Dinge. Der Diwan, die Apollokerzen und die Seele im technischen Zeitalter*, Berlin 2019

O'Donoghue, Diana, *On Dangerous Ground. Freud's Visual Cultures of the Unconscious*, New York 2019

Overbeck, Johannes, *Pompeji in seinen Gebäuden, Alterthümern und Kunstwerken für Kunst- und Alterthumsfreunde dargestellt*, Leipzig 1856

Pelz, Annegret, "Aufstellungen. Freuds Schreibtisch", in: *Freud und die Antike*, eds. Claudia Benthein, Hartmut Böhme & Inge Stephan, Göttingen 2011, pp. 51–68

Pessler, Monika, "Vienna, Berggasse 19. Seeing the centre ground", in: *Edmund Engelman. Sigmund Feud – Berggasse 19, Vienna*, (trans. Martin Kelsey), 5th edn Vienna 2016, pp. 7–18

Phillips, Adam, *On Kissing, Tickling, and Being Bored*, Cambridge, Mass., 1997

Pichler, Wolfram, Wener Rappl & Gudrun Swoboda, "Metamorphosen des Flussgottes und der Nymphe. Aby Warburgs Denk-Haltungen und die Psychoanalyse", in: *Die Couch. Vom Denken im Liegen*, ed. Lydia Marinelli, Munich, Berlin, London & New York 2006, pp. 161–86

Rank, Otto & Hanns Sachs, *Die Bedeutung der Psychoanalyse für die Geisteswissenschaften*, Wiesbaden 1913

Ransohoff, Rita, "Bildbeschreibungen", in: *Edmund Engelman, Berggasse 19. Das Wiener Domizil Sigmund Freuds*, Stuttgart & Zürich 1977, pp. 137–58

Raphael-Leff, Joan, "If Oedipus was an Egyptian", *The International Review of Psycho-analysis*, XVII (1990), pp. 309–25

Reiche, Reimut, *Mutterseelenallein. Kunst, Form und Psychoanalyse*, Frankfurt am Main & Basel 2001

The Revised Standard Edition of the Complete Psychological Works of Sigmund Freud, rev., enl. & ed. Mark Solms, 24 vols, Lanham, Md., & London 2024

Rice, Emanuel, *Freud and Moses. The Long Journey Home*, Albany, NY, 1990

Rolnik, Eran, "With this Ring: Art and Loyalty in the Freudian Circle", in: *Freud of the Rings*, exh. cat., ed. Morag Wilhelm, Jerusalem 2018, pp. 13–35

Rose, Louis, *The Survival of Images. Art Historians, Psychoanalysts, and the Ancients*, Detroit 2001

Rossini, Orietta, "Ludwig Pollak e Sigmund Freud. Un incontro ai confini della notte", in: *Ludwig Pollak. Archeologo e mercante d'arte. Praga 1868–Auschwitz 1943. Gli anni d'oro del collezionismo internazionale da Giovanni Barracco a Sigmund Freud*, ed. Orietta Rossini, Rome 2018a, pp. 148–61

Rossini, Orietta, "Ludwig Pollak. La vita e le opere", in: *Ludwig Pollak. Archeologo e mercante d'arte. Praga 1868–Auschwitz 1943. Gli anni d'oro del collezionismo internazionale da Giovanni Barracco a Sigmund Freud*, ed. Orietta Rossini, Rome 2018b, pp. 15–35

Rothauser, Max, "Der ungarische Büchmann", *Ungarische Revue*, XV / 1–2 (1895), pp. 97–103

Roudinesco, Élisabeth, *Freud in his Time*, Cambridge, Mass. 2016

Ruhs, August, "Hören, sprechen, liegen. Fauteuil und Couch", in: *Kino im Kopf. Psychologie und Film seit Sigmund Freud*, ed. Kristina Jaspers & Wolf Unterberger, Berlin 2006, pp. 53–58

Ruhs, August, "Die psychoanalytische Behandlungsmethode", in: *Freud, Berggasse 19. Ursprungsort der Psychoanalyse*, ed. Monika Pessler & Daniela Finzi, Berlin 2020, pp. 201–07

Sachs, Hanns, *Freud. Master and Friend*, London 1945

Sachsse, Rolf, "Max Halberstadt", *Hamburg History Live*, LI (2001), pp. 14–29

Sadger, Isidor, *Sigmund Freud. Persönliche Erinnerungen*, ed. Andrea Huppke & Michael Schröter, Tübingen 2006

Said, Edward W., *Freud and the Non-European*, London & New York 2003

Satzinger, Georg, "Michelangelos Grabmal Julius' II. in S. Pietro in Vincoli", *Zeitschrift für Kunstgeschichte*, LXIV / 2 (2001), pp. 177–222

Schäfer, Peter, "The Triumph of Pure Spirituality. Sigmund Freud's *Moses and Monotheism*", *Jewish Studies Quarterly*, IX / 4 (2002), pp. 381–406

Schäfer, Peter, *Der Triumph der reinen Geistigkeit. Sigmund Freuds "Der Mann Moses und die monotheistische Religion"*, Berlin & Vienna 2003

Schäfer, Peter, *Zwei Götter im Himmel. Gottesvorstellungen in der jüdischen Antike*, Munich 2017

Schlesier, Renata, "'Ungestraft unter Palmen', Freud in Italien". *Vorträge aus dem Warburg-Haus*, VIII (2004), pp. 167–98

Schmidbauer, Wolfgang, *Freuds Dilemma. Die Wissenschaft von der Seele und die Kunst der Therapie*, Reinbek bei Hamburg 1999

Schmidgen, Henning, *Horn oder Die Gegenseite der Medien*, Berlin 2018

Schorske, Carl E., *Fin-de-siècle Vienna: politics and culture*, London & New York 1980

Schorske, Carl E., "To the Egyptian Dig. Freud's Exploration in Western Culture", in: Schorske, Carl E., *Thinking with history. Explorations in the passage to modernism*, Princeton 1998, pp. 191–216

Schröter, Michael, *Auf eigenem Weg. Geschichte der Psychoanalyse in Deutschland bis 1945*, Göttingen 2023

Sears, Elizabeth, "Eye Training. Goldschmidt / Wölfflin", in: *Adolph Goldschmidt (1863–1944). Normal Art History im 20. Jahrhundert*, ed. Gunnar Brands & Heinrich Dilly, Weimar 2007, pp. 275–94

Settis, Salvatore, "Emanuel Löwy, fra Austria e Italia", in: *Römische historische Mitteilungen*, LVII (2015), pp. 121–30

SFG – Sigmund Freud Gesamtausgabe, ed. Christfried Tögel, with the assistance of Urban Zerfass, 23 vols, Giessen 2015–23

Simmons, Laurence, *Freud's Italian Journey*, Amsterdam & New York 2006

Spankie, Ro, *Sigmund Freud's Desk*, 3rd edn London 2019

Spector, Jack J., *The Aesthetics of Freud. A Study in Psychoanalysis and Art*, New York 1972

Spitteler, Carl, *Imago*, Jena 1906

Stadler, Ulrich, *Kafkas Poetik*, Zürich 2019

Stephan, Inge, "Nachstellungen. Die Antike im psychoanalytischen Alltag", in: *Freud und die Antike*, ed. Claudia Benthien, Harmut Böhme & Inge Stephan, Gottingen 2011, pp. 33–50

Stockreiter, Karl, "Am Rand der Aufklärungsmetapher. Korrespondenzen zwischen Archäologie und Psychoanalyse", in: *"Meine ... alten und dreckigen Götter". Aus Sigmund Freuds Sammlung*, exh. cat., ed. Lydia Marinelli, Vienna 1998, pp. 80–93

Tögel Christfried, *Berggasse – Pompeji und zurück. Sigmund Freuds Reisen in die Vergangenheit*, Tübingen 1989

Tögel, Christfried, *"... und gedenke die Wissenschaft auszubeuten". Sigmund Freuds Weg zur Psychoanalyse*, Tübingen 1994

Tögel, Christfried, "Gestern träumte ich wieder vom Reisen", in: *Sigmund Freud, Unser Herz zeigt nach dem Süden. Reisebriefe 1895–1923*, ed. Christfried Tögel, with the assistance of Michael Molnar, Berlin 2003, pp. 9–36

Tögel, Christfried, *Freud und Berlin*, Berlin 2006

Tögel, Christfried, "Fröhliche Wissenschaft – Zufallsfunde und ein Antiquitätenhändler", *Luzifer-Amor. Zeitschrift zur Geschichte der Psychoanalyse*, XXIV / 47 (2011). pp. 55–58

Tögel, Christfried, *Die Rätsel Sigmund Freuds. Von den Geschlechtsorganen des Aals zur Traumdeutung*, Giessen 2013

Tögel, Christfried, *Freuds Wien. Eine biografische Skizze nach Schauplätzen*, 2nd rev. & enl. edn Giessen 2015

Tögel, Christfried, "Freud, die Couch und Familie Benevisti", *Luzifer-Amor. Zeitschrift zur Geschichte der Psychoanalyse*, XXX / 59 (2017), pp. 171–73

Tögel, Christfried, *Alles über Freud*, Berlin 2019

Tögel, Christfried, *Freud wider Gott oder Die Stimme des Intellekts ist leise ...*, Vienna & Berlin 2024

Trotha, Hans von, *Pollaks Arm*, Berlin 2021

Tylor, Edward Burnett, *Primitive Culture*, 2 vols, London 1871, 1873

Tylor, Edward Burnett, *Die Anfänge der Cultur. Untersuchungen über die Entwicklung der Mythologie, Philosophie, Religion, Kunst und Sitte*, trans. J. W. Sprengel & F. Poske, 2 vols, Leipzig 1873

Ucko, Peter, "Unprovenanced Material Culture and Freud's Collection of Antiquities", *Journal of Material Culture*, VI / 3 (2001), pp. 209–322

Urban, Bernd & Johannes Cremerius, "Einleitung", in: *Sigmund Freud, Der Wahn und die Träume in W. Jensens "Gradiva", mit dem Text der Erzählung von Wilhelm Jensen*, Frankfurt am Main 1973, pp. 7–20

Vasari, Giorgio, *Le Vite de' più eccellenti pittori, scultori e architettori*, 2nd edn, 3 vols, Florence 1568

Verspohl, Franz-Joachim, "Michelangelo und Machiavelli. Der David auf der Piazza della Signoria in Florenz", in: *Städel-Jahrbuch*, new series VIII (1981), pp. 204–46

Verspohl, Franz-Joachim, "Der Moses des Michelangelo", in: *Städel-Jahrbuch*, new series, XIII (1991), pp. 155–76

Verspohl, Franz-Joachim, *Michelangelo Buonarroti und Niccolò Machiavelli*, Bern & Vienna 2001

Verspohl, Franz-Joachim, *Michelangelo Buonarroti und Papst Julius II. Moses – Heerführer, Gesetzgeber, Musenlenker*, Göttingen & Berlin 2004

Völkel, Henner, "Nachruf auf Prof. Dr. E. Störring (1903–2000) (available online at: https://studiengesellschaft.de/nachruf-auf-prof-dr-gustav-e-stoerring-1903-2000)

Warburg, Aby, *Briefe*, eds. Michael Diers, Steffen Haug & Thomas Helbig, Berlin & Boston 2021 (= *Aby Warburgs Gesammelte Schriften: Studienausgabe*, vol. V.1)

Ward, Ivan, "Freud's Chair and Desk", in: *Freud's Sculpture*, exh, cat., ed. Penelope Curtis & Jon Wood, Leeds 2006, pp. 27–37

Weiss, Heinz, "Pompeji und das Problem der Zeitlichkeit bei Freud", in: *Freud und die Antike*, ed. Claudia Benthien, Hartmut Böhme & Inge Stephan, Göttingen 2011, pp. 143–58

Weiss, Heinz & Carina Weiss, "Eine Welt wie im Traum – Sigmund Freud als Sammler antiker Kunstgegenstände", in: *Jahrbuch der Psychoanalyse. Beiträge zur Theorie, Praxis und Geschichte*, vol. XVI (1984), pp. 189–217

Weissweiler, Eva, *Die Freuds. Biographie einer Familie*, Cologne 2006

Werbőczi, István, *Tripartitum opus iuris consuetudinarij inclyti regni Hungariae*, Vienna 1517

Whitebook, Joel, *Freud. An Intellectual Biography*, Cambridge, New York & Melbourne

Wohlfart, Günter & Johann Kreuzer, "Schweigen, Stille", in: *Historisches Wörterbuch der Philosophie*, ed. Joachim Ritter, Karlfried Gründer & Gottfried Gabriel, vol. VIII (1992), cols 1493–95

Wolf, Harald, "Archäologische Freundschaften. Emamuel Löwys und Ludwig Pollaks Bedeutung für den Sammler Freud", in: *"Meine ... alten und dreckigen Götter". Aus Sigmund Freuds Sammlung*, exh. cat., ed. Lydia Marinelli, Vienna 1998, pp. 60–71

Wood. Jon, "Re-staging Freud's Sculpture", in: *Freud's Sculpture*, exh. cat., ed. Penelope Curtis & Jon Wood, Leeds 2006, pp. 5–17

Wörterbuch der philosophischen Begriffe, ed. Armin Regenbogen & Uwe Meyer, Hamburg 2013

Yerushalmi, Yosef Hayim, *Freud's Moses. Judaism Terminable and Interminable*, New Haven & London 1991

Zapperi, Roberto, *Alle Wege führen nach Rom. Die ewige Stadt und ihre Besucher*, Munich 2013

Zapperi, Roberto, *Freud und Mussolini*, Berlin 2016

INDEX

In this listing Sigmund Freud is referred to throughout as SF. All references to "psychoanalysis" denote that of the sort he devised and further developed.

PICTURE CREDITS

The principal information on each of the items and images illustrated as Figs. 1–49 is stated within its own caption. Those items and images also protected by copyright, museum copyright or photographic copyright, or for which the source was another publication, are listed below.

Fig. 1: © Freud Museum London
Fig. 2: published in Bredekamp 2021a, p. 575
Fig. 3: published in Bredekamp 2021a, p. 578
Fig. 4: © Freud Museum London
Fig. 5: author's archive
Fig. 6: Jörg Bittner Unna, CC BY 3.0, https://creativecommons.org/licenses/by/3.0, via Wikimedia Commons
Fig. 7: public domain, Sigmund Freud Papers, Library of Congress, Washington, D. C.
Fig. 8: public domain, Sigmund Freud Papers, Library of Congress, Washington, D. C.
Fig. 9: public domain, Sigmund Freud Papers, Library of Congress, Washington, D. C.
Fig.10: public domain, Kupferstichkabinett der Akademie der bildenden Künste, Vienna
Fig. 11: © Sigmund Freud Papers, Library of Congress, Washington. D. C.
Fig. 12: public domain, Österreichische Nationalbibliothek, Vienna
Fig. 13: published in Bredekamp 2021a, p. 578
Fig. 14: published in Freud (1914), pp. 28–29
Fig. 15: published in Lermolieff (1890), p. 98
Fig. 16: published in Dennis (1878), p. 68
Fig. 17: published in Molnar (1998), p. 40
Fig. 18: © Bibliotheca Hertziana, Rome, U. Pl. B 88
Fig. 19: published in Mambelli, Francesca, 'À Reproduire', in: *Mitteilungen des Kunsthistorischen Institutes in Florenz*, LXII / 1 (2020), pp. 11–41, here 17
Fig. 20: published in Engelman (1993), p. 23
Fig. 21: modified ground plan based on that in *Freud, Berggasse 19: Ursprungsort der Psychoanalyse* (2020), p. 138
Fig. 23 left: published in Engelman (1993), pp. 38–39
Fig. 24 left: published in Engelman (2016), pp. 48–49
Fig. 25 left: published in Engelman (1977a), p. 91
Fig. 26 left: published in Engelman (2016), pp. 54–55
Fig. 27 left: published in Engelman (1993), p. 60
Fig. 28 left: published in Engelman (2016), p. 60

Fig. 29 left: published in Engelman (2016), p. 68
Fig. 30 left: published in Engelman (2016), p. 36
Fig. 31 left: published in Engelman (2016), p. 37
Fig. 32 left: published in Engelman (2016), p. 33
Fig. 33: © Freud Museum London
Fig. 34: © Freud Museum London
Fig. 35: © Freud Museum London
Fig. 36: © Freud Museum London
Fig. 37: © Freud Museum London
Fig. 38: © Freud Museum London
Fig. 39: © Freud Museum London
Fig. 40: © Freud Museum London
Fig. 41: © Freud Museum London
Fig. 42: published in Engelman (1977a), p. 97
Fig. 43 left: published in Engelman (2016), p. 47
Fig. 44 left: published in Engelman (2016), p. 39
Fig. 45: public domain, via Wikimedia Commons
Fig. 46: public domain, via Wikimedia Commons
Fig. 47: © Freud Museum London
Fig. 48: published in Aurnhammer / von den Hoff (2022), p. 166
Fig. 49: © Freud Museum London